THERE IS
ALWAYS
HOPE

——— *Your Story Matters* ———
Stories to Stir Your Soul with Lasting HOPE

PUBLISHED BY THE

INTERNATIONAL
SCHOOL
OF STORY

Library of Congress Cataloging-in-Publication Data
Smith, Emra 1959
There is Always Hope

Library of Congress Control Number: 2017905184
ISBN: 978-1-942923-24-4 (paperback)

THERE IS
ALWAYS
HOPE

—————— *Your Story Matters* ——————
Stories to Stir Your Soul with Lasting HOPE

EMRA SMITH

For, You, the reader.
Because You Matter.
Immensely.
Always.
For eternity.

Contents

Introduction

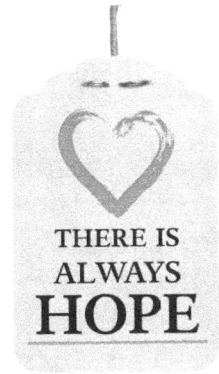

THERE IS
ALWAYS
HOPE

We all have stories to tell. To experience life is to be conscious of one another's story, and to share our stories with others. There are glorious moments that are easy to share and there are times that challenge us and leave us feeling depleted. We tend to hold the challenging moments inside our hearts, hiding them from the world.

We can choose to allow our stories to grow us, or destroy us. Our stories define us. We can understand and work through our stories in such a way that they refine us, revealing the treasure we are becoming. Through sharing our stories, we are empowered, encouraged, and strengthened. Sharing our stories impacts us and others. Our stories could potentially change the way someone else views the world.

Through many experiences in my life, without a doubt, my sustaining power has come from my relationship and trust in God, and His ability to hold onto me. God has developed and blessed me with five essential life skills, or tools, to give me strength through some of the toughest times of my life. If I had understood the purpose of the life skills sooner, and practiced them with more consistency, I know I could have made wiser decisions and caused less pain to others and myself on the journey of life.

As a result of my hindsight epiphany, I feel compelled to share the essential skills with anyone who is willing to learn. I've chosen to share these tools in *There is Always HOPE*, the second book in *The Teatime Stories Collection*.

The purpose of *The Teatime Stories Collection* is to challenge you to *"be more, live more, and love more"* in God's purpose for your life. As you pursue the call, you will find peace that passes understanding. We need to remember, God recognizes the importance of our stories.

The first book in *The Teatime Stories Collection* is *Your Story Matters*, which shares the essence of why your story matters. Each *Teatime* book provides proof that God has a plan for each of our lives, surpassing our wildest dreams.

The book in your hands, *There is Always HOPE*, is divided into five sections—one section for each Life Skill. The stories of HOPE in each section reflect the power of the corresponding skill as applied to the challenges and life experiences women endure. You will see the power of God and how He impacted the lives of each of the spotlighted women.

An important ingredient to living an empowered life is maintaining HOPE as we face life's challenges and grow through them. One of the most efficient ways to ignite and strengthen our HOPE is through knowing the stories of others who have gone before us. Through their example, we find the inspiration, strength, and courage to answer the call to fulfill our purpose and *"be more, live more, and love more."*

My prayer for each of you is that your soul would

be stirred to choose one or more of the Five Essential Life Skills to implement your God-given purpose. May your heart be filled with HOPE, faith, and courage. Know you CAN do all things through Christ who strengthens you.

May you choose
to impact the world with
His story through yours.

With love and a prayer for you in my heart,

Emra

Cease the busy.
Change the hurried cup of coffee
For a soothing cup of tea.
Get comfy.
Sink into a favorite chair.
Sip and be soul-stirred as never before.
Be empowered.

Receive HOPE through these stories.

Have faith.
Have courage.
Gain strength.

YOU ARE NOT ALONE

YOUR Story Matters.
Each story matters.
The big stories.
The little stories.
Each one, every day.
Your entire life matters.
You matter.

"Do you not know?
Have you not heard?
The Everlasting God,
The Lord,
The Creator of the ends of the earth
Does not become weary or tired.
His understanding is inscrutable.
He gives strength to the weary,
And to him who lacks might
He increases power."

Isaiah 40:28-29 (NASB)

My Story
Living, Learning & Loving Life to the Full

Emra Smith

THERE IS
ALWAYS
HOPE

"I have come that you may have life and have it to the full."
Jesus, in John 10:10

Join me. Let's sit lazily on the porch rockers at The House of Story. It's a gentle summer's day, and the scent of fresh rain-washed trees and blooms waft on the sprawling deck. A woodpecker hammers and hummingbirds dart to and fro. After a long mellow moment, I swirl my favorite teaspoon in my teacup and watch as the tea twirls in your direction, just as our stories stir our souls.

• • •

I was the quiet child from a broken home, raised bilingual with an unusual blend of religions. I was the odd one out that never really fit in anywhere, born in Krugersdorp, South Africa. My mom left me with my dad until I was three years old. That's when she returned and abruptly whisked me off to Johannesburg and her new marriage.

Three years later, my new dad's daughter moved in with us too. Mom's efforts to please her mother-in-law, who disliked her, went awry and our house became turbulent. I would hide and cry out in fear to a God I did not know, asking Him to calm my mom down as she poured her anger out on my step-sister.

My first language was Afrikaans, but I also spoke English. I attended a small, private English school before transferring to a much larger, all-girls Afrikaans high school.

I struggled to find my feet in my new environment. The religion my mom adopted was different from that of my peers. The fact that I was vegetarian, attended church on Saturdays, and kept some Jewish Holidays, only intensified the effect of my "sticking out like a sore thumb." I also looked nothing like the other girls with my head full of curls. To my surprise, the girls loved me, and I became the "go-to" friend others shared their problems with and sought out for advice.

Somehow, this duality of being the outsider, both at school and at home, gave me the space I needed to be still, think, and dream. As I twirled and danced clumsily in the garden, I'd picture myself being a movie star, a writer, or a speaker that changed the whole world and made it a better place.

I started speaking and teaching at church for my peers as well as coaching my friends at school. That's when I decided I would be a psychologist when I went off to college.

My plans changed when I fell in love.

I longed for freedom and the adventure of being a grown-up, so I married at twenty-one. We moved after the wedding, and I passionately lived for the day at hand. My strong faith helped me believe we could achieve whatever we desired. I gave up my studies and poured myself into growing my husband's optometry practice.

I didn't ponder for one moment about my childhood dreams, and succumbed, for the most part, to my husband's desires and life goals. I didn't realize it at the time, but my childhood dreams were still locked inside of me, along with energy and zest for life.

Shortly after our first anniversary, our amazing daughter was born. Those first few years were tough for me. I felt lost and alone in a man's world I had no real interest in. I had to learn to cook, keep house, and raise a baby—all of which I wasn't prepared for.

All I wanted was to conquer the world and make it a better place, but I couldn't even conquer my life. Despite the reality of my life, I *never complained*, even to myself. I accepted that my life was how it was supposed to be.

Even though it took me awhile to adjust to being a mom, three years later I was excited to find out I was pregnant again. In my blissful excitement, I had no way of knowing what lay ahead after our new, tiny daughter's birth. The weeks slipped into months as I moved through each day in a fog of exhaustion. I fed my little baby every two hours, night and day, while trying to keep up with my toddler and the rest of life.

When I noticed my second daughter was not reaching the milestones other babies do, I went to the pediatrician. The doctor said she was merely a "slow developer."

Following the advice of friends, I took my child for another opinion and was referred to a school for children with Cerebral Palsy to see a physical therapist. That heartbreaking day began my journey of coming to terms with the fact that my child was physically challenged.

Six years later, a doctor friend in the USA urged us to see a geneticist. We did as he suggested. Within two minutes of being in the geneticist's office, he said, "Cornelia de Lange Syndrome."

He explained the syndrome and how rare it was in South Africa. He then connected us with a foundation in America. To this day, I still remember how I felt when we left his office. It felt as if I had entered a vast, black vacuum. I was numb. My world was cold and deathly quiet.

The months and years that followed seemed like a whirlwind. My husband didn't like to speak about our daughter's condition to anyone, so I began an internal journey of confusion and complexities. People around me glared with judgment; they didn't understand why I couldn't control Candi's behavior. Her therapists would reprimand me for not working hard enough with her. My mother couldn't handle being around, which caused her already infrequent visits to become almost nonexistent.

I never found a support group, and for several years, I soldiered on quietly, *never complaining*, but also not taking the time to reflect. I completely ignored my needs, which seemed to go unnoticed by everyone around me.

I remember the day I realized my energy, joy, courage, and strength were depleted. It felt as if I was about to "snap" and lose my mind. I ran to my room, shut the door, and fell on my knees. From a deep, hollow space inside, I sobbed before God.

All I could say was, "Help me. Help me." I don't know how long I knelt in anguish there. It could have been a minute, or maybe an hour. What I do know is, after that moment great peace filled me.

I stood up with a spring in my step, renewed strength, courage, and a smile on my face. Nothing around me had changed, but I had changed. My spirituality was my anchor. It would not be the last time I would find myself on the verge of breaking and find God still sustaining me.

Even through the God-moments where I found strength, I still did not take time to pause, reflect, practice self-care, or gain understanding about what was depleting me or how to stop it.

I decided to focus my sheer willpower on changing my outlook. I was determined to laugh and find joy, believing to my core that each day in life counts. I committed to making the most of life. I would take my eldest daughter, Lianro, to tea, We loved to go out together. I focused on her young life—ballet lessons, swimming, sleepovers. There were girls everywhere.

I invested some time in studying and researching about *healthy living* and plunged the family into eating a super healthy diet. I started running and found my quiet, peace, and vitality in those moments. My coping skills served me well and gave me a sense of control in my chaotic life that kept me sane.

I spent much of my time serving at our church. I worked with the teens and women, which gave me joy and energy. I started a food sharing program with the children of the inner city. I found that looking outside of myself and *giving* to others brought a joy that sustained me.

As my husband's business expanded, he began to yearn for change and his desire to move to America grew. My heart was torn. I had gone to many seminars in America and devoured all I could learn. I also had two mentors I loved who lived there, and the thought of having them in my life brought a smile of comfort. But, my love of my country—its smells, colors, music, and people—deeply filled my soul.

I knew that America would give my girls a great future, especially Candi, who could learn to live independently and experience life in a way she never could in South Africa. It was upon this realization that I knew I had to go, for them and their future. In 1996, we left South Africa and began our journey toward what we prayed would be a brighter future.

We moved to Maryland where Homer Optical Company hired me as the Director of Marketing. It was scary and beautiful as I stepped into a space where I could explore and excel. I vividly remember feeling overwhelmed in my office, not knowing whether I would succeed or not. Then I remember experiencing a calm presence that washed over me. The Holy Spirit impressed me saying, "Just be yourself. Do what you've always done." I did just that and cared for the customers, trained the staff to do the same, and I saw the business turn around. I loved corporate America and dreamed of greatness for my family.

Through all of the joy, a deep sense of loss and grief for my friends, family, and homeland weaved into each day. Church became a painful place to be, and hot tears would stream down my cheeks as I pictured those I loved in South Africa. The complexities of immigrating and the impact on our family was as icy as the freezing weather. I often wanted to stop everything and just scream. I realize now that I should have, yet I kept it all inside, as I always had.

Dark years followed what started out as a bright transition. My mom died unexpectedly at sixty-five, and I was unable to return to South Africa for her funeral. I quickly burned out of love for America and wanted to leave. I felt I had little left to give. Through the years, I never learned to take care of me, and, in the absence of all things familiar, I had finally run dry.

I found the warmth and affection I sought in the comfort of another man who seemed to be my only friend. I shared my heart and anguish with him, causing the gulf of separation in my marriage to widen.

In a desperate effort to save our marriage, we moved our little family to the Florida Keys to help my mentors with their non-profit organization. Life began to take on a quieter pace, and the family was, seemingly, together again. I didn't realize how saying goodbye to my job at the company I had grown to love would add to the unbearable weight of increasing loss burdening me.

I hated our new home and resented having to move, but my core belief in the importance of each day kept me going. I had my love of life, laughter, and my girls to help me find beauty in each day. I fell in love with the color of the water and moved on with my life as best as I could.

The turmoil and joy of raising Candi became an intricate part of each day, as did the struggle to find our financial feet. Our money quickly depleted, so I started two small businesses to survive, selling art and doing yard work. I did anything I could to make ends meet.

My husband and I each had such unique skills. Unfortunately, instead of working together by complimenting each other and building a strong business, we always argued and could never seem to agree on anything. Soon after moving to Florida, our green cards were set to expire. We made numerous attempts to renew them, but they kept denying my husband's extension. We had one last hope before our visas expired.

My mentor's husband, Merlin, found us a new lawyer and urged—almost dragged—me along to the appointment. Had I not gone, we would never have known that I could get the green cards for the family.

My giving and service for God in South Africa that began again in the Florida Keys met the requirements. I realized, once again, that you can never out-give God and that sharing one's gifts with the world not only blesses others, but returns to you in unknown ways.

God made a way for my family that I would never have thought to ask for. I will never forget the wave of relief that washed over me when they approved our cards. That moment would only be surpassed by the relief I felt when I became an American citizen.

Years later, still living in America, I discovered for the first time the history of what transpired in my homeland while I was growing up. We had no freedom of the press. My non-political family did not talk much about current events. Apartheid disbanded by the time I was an adult, so I had no idea at all about anything that had occurred. My grief upon learning the truth of the horrors that happened overwhelmed me, but that is a story for another book.

I have many beautiful and sad stories that happened in the years between the Florida Keys and our lives today. I will have to share those details over another cup of tea one day. They're stories about the gift of my dream house, my first published book, and Arthur—my American Dad.

There were many gifts, pains, and sorrows of friends gained and lost. I could tell about my adventures in art and small business, or about becoming a corporate trainer in the hospitality industry. I could share about how I sought warmth and affection from father figures that filled the empty space my biological father left in me.

The story that all of these circumstances and situations revolved around was inside me, not external. The vicious cycle of pouring myself out serving others, expecting to find fulfillment, but finding emptiness in its place, had never ceased. In an effort to break the cycle, and going against every core value I had, I chose divorce after twenty-five years.

I hurt my eldest daughter and broke my husband's heart in the process, which almost destroyed me. My choice will forever be a pivotal point in my life. I didn't want to live anymore, so I fled from God.

The beauty that came from this heartbreaking decision was that I finally learned to invest in me and take care of myself. What an arduous journey I chose to come to a seemingly simple realization.

I went to counseling for nine months as I struggled with life being single. I married my friend, Roberdy, a year later. He was the vessel God used to teach me the essence of respect, a lesson I deeply treasure.

In my new season, I allowed myself to become as vulnerable and open as a child again. I brought my raw emotions, thoughts, and honest complaints before God. I allowed Him to re-create me as He intended me to be. I sought to see myself as He has always seen me. Absent from the voices, demands, and cares of others, I opened myself to learning about who God created me to be.

In the process, I learned to *affirm myself.* I learned the art of *not complaining,* which is different than the act of pretending nothing is wrong. It was, rather, a conscious effort to pause, take stock, and make changes while placing what could not change in God's capable hands.

Little by little, I unfolded, no longer a stranger to myself. I had to wrestle through forgiveness on many levels, letting go of bitterness I didn't know I was harboring. I became a certified Life Coach and soared to the other side with my Mentor, Coach Dr. Dave Krueger.

Much joy and excitement followed my transformation. I became a grandma, started a business, and embraced my gifts, my work, and what I have to share with the world. I am now living a *purpose-filled* life of *giving.*

My sustaining power, without a doubt, has come from my relationship and belief in God, and His ability to hold onto me. If I had understood the purpose sooner, and practiced these skills with more consistency, I know I could have made wiser decisions and caused less pain to others and myself in the journey I have taken.

My prayer is that you . . .

Allow the stories in this book, and the Five Essential Life Skills to challenge you to *live more, be more and love more* in your God-given purpose.

Pause and reflect on your life to see where you may need healing, assess missing aspects, and make wiser choices.

Allow your courage, strength, and hope soar.

Know that *Your Story Matters.*

Believe God has a story to tell through your story and determine to step into it. Here lies your joy. Your peace.

"I have told you these things,
so that in Me you may have peace.
In the world you will have trouble.
But take heart, I have overcome the world."
John 16:33 (NIV)

"The purpose of life is to live it,
to taste experience to the utmost.
To reach out eagerly and
without fear for
newer and richer experience."
Eleanor Roosevelt

God can bring
Peace to your past
Purpose to you present
And HOPE to your future.

The Five Essentials
Life Changing Skills that Bring Hope

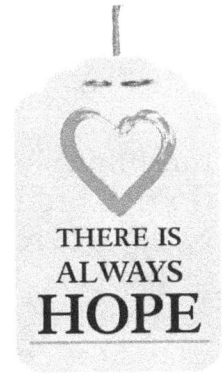

THERE IS
ALWAYS
HOPE

Here are the Five Essential Life Skills you need to live out God's story through yours. They are practical skills that, if under girded by time spent in prayer and building a solid relationship with God, will result in deep inner joy and peace.

1. **DON'T WHINE—WIN!** No complaining. Take responsibility and choose what is right for you.
Take responsibility for your life and make wise choices that align within your core values, spiritual gifts, needs, and wants. "No complaining" doesn't mean you pretend nothing bad is happening, but that you pause, take note, and choose change, or not. Then, do not complain about your choice.
Look for creative ways to live powerfully in your change. Neuroscience and Quantum Physics prove we receive what we focus on, not what we want. Focus aligns the energy field of the brain to direct our attention and effort. If you're focused on complaining, the very thing you complain about engulfs you, creating the reality you wish wasn't so.

2. AFFIRMATIONS, THANKSGIVING, & PRAISE.
Learn to see your strengths and how God created you. Be grateful. Affirmations are stories that revise

the mind's software and support rewiring the brain. God's Word tells us, "For as he thinks within himself, so he is." Proverbs 23:7 (NASB)

Romans 12:2 tells us to be transformed by the renewing of our minds. 2 Corinthians 10:5 commands us to take every thought captive.

With God's help, do the work needed to affirm yourself and your God-given strengths. Be honest, refocus, and live out who God created you to be.

Turn your affirmations into THANKSGIVING and PRAISE, giving God the glory for making you who you are.

3. Choose a HEALTHY LIFESTYLE by taking care of your physical body. Your body is your only vehicle. It will either deplete or energize you. Along with the physical, a healthy lifestyle also encompasses the mental, emotional, and spiritual part of your being. The first two skills profoundly impact your mental, emotional, and spiritual aspects, as can the physical state of your body.

4. Understand and know your God-given PURPOSE, bringing your DREAMS to Him. Allow Him to give you assignments and turn them into GOALS and ACTIONS. Be unattached to your timeline and open to His unexpected twists and turns.

5. Practice the art of GIVING and FORGIVING. Give to yourself and God. Allow your giving to others to be appropriate, and long lasting.

*Refresh your tea,
stretch you legs
and be prepared
to be inspired,
stimulated,
and called to action
by the stories that follow.*

"See I am doing a new thing."
Isaiah 43:19 (AMP)

DON'T WHINE
WIN!

*No Complaining.
Taking responsibility and
choosing what's right for you.*

Don't Whine—Win!
No Complaining! Taking Responsibility &
Choosing What is Right for You.

THERE IS
ALWAYS
HOPE

*"Death and life are in the power of the tongue,
and those who love it will eat its fruit."*
Proverbs 18:21 (ESV)

There are powerful benefits for everyday life if you embrace the wisdom of Proverbs! You will reap what you sow. Your words affect those around you and yourself. You impact your daily life as you set yourself up for failure or success through your thoughts, which become words and actions.

"For as he thinks within himself, so is he." Proverbs 23:7 (NASB)

As you complain, you reinforce a negative mindset and experience. As you hold negative thoughts and words in your heart, your days become filled with misery. You assume a victim mentality. You lose your personal power. With each thought, you wire your brain, establish behavior, and determine the life you live. Equally so, if you bury the difficulties in your life that trouble you and pretend they're not there, the toxins accumulate, and you will experience severe consequences.

Instead of complaining, be honest and ask God to reveal what's hidden in your heart. Share with Him your aggravations, hatred, hurt, pain, and all that troubles you. Listen to what He says, and deal with the root of what troubles you. It's often difficult to make sense of what is going on inside, but we know we must find resolution to move forward.

You cannot overcome problems alone. Ask God to lead you to a coach, a pastor, a counselor, or a trusted prayer warrior. Through these vessels of healing and wisdom, you can experience the miracle of change He will create for you.

"Therefore, preparing your minds for action, and being sober-minded, set your HOPE fully on the grace that will be brought to you at the revelation of Jesus Christ." 1 Peter 1:13 (ESV)

You cannot stay in a place of blaming others or your environment for your complexities. Sometimes it is really tough not to blame because hurt and pain can come to you through no fault of your own; however, you need to take full responsibility for every action you take. One of the choices you can make is to choose forgiveness and peace, even when life is unfair. It is always YOUR CHOICE as to how you respond.

Choose to CHANGE or ACCEPT the situation you're in, and deal with the consequences either way. Remember the rule: NO COMPLAINING! After contemplating the possible experience and the outcomes, make your choice, and own it. Understand why you chose what you did and the reasons for it. Taking responsibility will help you to remind yourself what you wanted and why, when you are tempted to complain.

You may catch yourself falling into your pattern of complaining the first week, but don't become discouraged; just start again. It takes time to form a new habit. Complaining is merely a habit. It is a destructive habit that doesn't make anything better. It steals your joy and makes peace an elusive experience.

"What you're supposed to do when you
don't like a thing is change it.
If you can't change it,
change the way you think about it.
Don't complain."

Maya Angelou
Wouldn't Take Nothing for My Journey Now

Celebrating Grace
Don't Whine—Win!

Holly Dowling

THERE IS
ALWAYS
HOPE

I briefly saw Holly Dowling at the EBW2020 Women's Retreat and through the sisterhood's regular Facebook communication became an eager listener to her new podcast series, A Celebration of You. Her soothing, energizing, and embracing voice drew me in; I knew she was a woman of substance. Our connection grew when she interviewed me for her podcast, and our hearts became one. "Holly-isms" strike to the core, stick with you and bring hope and courage.

• • •

It is easy to become lost in the dark clouds of life, but we don't have to stay there. I choose not to live in a perpetual "woe is me," but rather to live in a "wow is me" mentality! I have found that choosing joy leaves me with no tolerance for whining and enables me to share the grace God has so lavishly poured into my many stories.

I was the first of four siblings born to my Mayflower-descendant mother and Teheran-born father. They were both disowned from their families because of their marriage.

I used to be the overweight, shy little girl who endured incessant teasing, but secretly, I was strong. I had many dreams and aspirations even as a child. As a third grader, I started my first business.

While watching *The Love Boat*, I dreamt that some day I would grow up to be like Julie, as she was everything I desired to be. Then, I unexpectedly met Jesus at a "Youth for Christ" camp and realized God loved me just as I was.

My eyes were still set on traveling the world as my dad pushed me to finish a college degree. As the final day of classes drew closer, I embarked on what everyone thought was an impossible quest. I decided to create a job for myself that would allow me to travel the world doing what I loved. I began to scour travel magazines for names of cruise ships to pitch my ideas to. I sent out 19 hot pink folders with cover letters and resumes, learned to speak French, and even set up meetings with travel agents. Everyone told me my dream wouldn't happen.

"Tell me no and watch me go!" My mantra carried me through the obstacles that came before achieving my dream. Within one month, I was off and on my way to be the Social and Sports Hostess aboard American Hawaii Cruise Ships in Tahiti. I never let go of my dream, never stopped believing it could happen, and I did my fair share of hard work to see it come to pass. After I was hired, I even sent a thank you note to each person that discouraged me or denied my application. My note read: "Thank you for your time. I am about to set sail on the SS Liberte."

My cruise ship adventure ended when the company closed its doors. I checked my cruise ship dream off my bucket list and moved on to my next adventure. I wanted to work at a resort. I found a job at St. John in the Virgin Islands, where I helped open the guest services department.

I was just shy of a year working at St. John and had great opportunities ahead. Then a relationship I began in college resurfaced, and I chose to come back home. Before going to college, I was a virgin, never drank, and had clear boundaries for myself. In college, I made a dark turn toward partying and became involved with the BMOC (Big Man On Campus). I set my faith aside and those years quickly became one of the ugliest times of my life. The relationship had an undercurrent of slight abuse, which I didn't understand or see at the time. I allowed the influence and will of another person to impact my choices.

For 488 days, I allowed my boyfriend to curse at me and call me demeaning names. He compared me to a female dog and made me feel inferior. Then the abuse transitioned from verbal to physical. I was too embarrassed to tell anyone how my homecoming queen life had turned into a nightmare. I hid in my shoe closet most nights, where God protected me.

One evening, as I stood in front of a mirror, I didn't recognize the person looking back at me. I heard an angel sent by the grace of God say to me, "You're beautiful, and you have a huge life ahead." It was the word of hope I needed. Instantly, I knew I had to escape. I ran outside, barefoot in my PJs in three feet of snow, and climbed a tree. I watched the house and waited for my boyfriend to leave. Once he was gone, I got in my car with only the clothes on my back and drove to another state where I stayed in a safe place for three days before moving into a home.

I started a new life for myself, baffled at how I could have gone from living a high life to going to such a low place. How did it all happen to me? It took me years of therapy to understand. My faith brought me through and, after 15 years, I could talk about it.

It was almost twenty-eight years before I healed enough to share my story. I had to learn to forgive and to let go of resentment so I could become who I am today. In my dark place, I found opportunities to grow and believe. Without my faith, I would have died inside and shut myself off from the world.

I became involved in Bible studies a few years ago and was asked to share my story at the local high school. I had never done anything like that before, but I was willing despite my apprehension. When I stepped out, God stepped in.

I spoke about having dreams and tucking them under your pillow. Humans will always let you down, but if you know God loves you, you can get through life. After I had spoken, a high school boy came up to me and said, "I don't want to do what my dad does. He abuses my mom and me, and I now see it in me too."

That young man's statement left me feeling a boldness. I saw the impact I made on the teen, and the next thing I knew, I was speaking at an assembly in the auditorium to all the students and parents. One parent came up to me and asked if I would speak in a corporate environment. I said yes, and an entire platform opened before me. Saying "Yes" to God that first time opened doors I never dreamed possible for my witness to expand.

I have always seized opportunities instead of waiting for them to come to me and I've had many wonderful experiences as a result. For example, *The Summit of Eight*, more commonly know as the G8 Summit, was going to take place in my city. *The Summit* is an assembly of national leaders from eight of the world's most prominent countries. The leaders come together to address current issues in government, economics, global security, and other relevant worldwide topics.

I boldly asked the planning committee how the city was preparing for the event and offered my business services. (I literally created my offering of business services that very moment). My creativity and willingness opened the door for me to be involved at *The Summit*.

After that, global speaking opportunities began unfolding. I saw myself as God's messenger; I would never hold back or be ashamed to show my audience who I am and why my message is relevant. The world needs to know where our strength and life comes from—God. The invites to speak have continued to flow in ever since I made a choice to be obedient to God and was willing to step out by faith.

I always thought my circle of influence would be limited to the Christian world, but I heard God's voice say to me, "No, I need you in the secular world." I began to branch out and make myself available to secular circles, and as a result, I have traveled extensively all over the world for companies like IBM, Deloitte, Facebook, Gap Brands, etc. I'm passionate about sharing the message of strength that God has given to me. As a partner of Marcus Buckingham, I have had the opportunity to speak to numerous authors that have written about topics that align with my beliefs, heart, and passion.

Through these years of ministering and speaking life into others, God wove in the gift and blessing of a family. He gave me many more reasons to believe in and trust Him. Along with all of the blessings there have been dark clouds too, which have also brought me closer to God.

My eldest child was diagnosed with a rare form of cancer at age two. The diagnosis occurred around the same time my second son was born. We didn't have the finances to pay for treatment, but miraculously a doctor offered us a trial drug, free of charge. Despite the bleak diagnosis, my son survived and is now a healthy, 25-year-old.

We were told that as a result of the trial drug treatment he would never have children. But, God is still the healer, and my son gave me my little grandson! That's just two examples of miracles of light that came shining out from the midst of woe.

Wow is me! What a gift to live a life celebrating the God who gives us life and empowers us in spite of circumstances. What a privilege to seek and see the "wow" and not the "woe" in life!

• • •

To learn more about Holly visit HollyDowling.com. Listen to Holly's podcast, *A Celebration of You*, on iTunes.

For Prayerful Application

1. Do you live in "woe is me" or do you choose the "wow" is me?

"Are you tired? Worn out? Burned out on Religion?
Come to Me, and you'll recover your life.
I'll show you how to take real rest.
Walk with me and work with Me – watch how I do it.
Learn the unforced rhythms of grace.
I won't lay anything heavy or ill-fitting on you.
Keep company with me,
and You'll learn to live freely and lightly."
Matthew 11:28-30 (MSG)

2. Are you afraid to step out and share your story or share Jesus as your source of power and life?

"You're my servant, serving on My side. I've picked you. I
haven't dropped you. Don't panic. I'm with you. There's no
need to fear for I'm your God. I'll give you strength. I'll help
you. I'll hold you steady, keep a firm grip on you."
Isaiah 42:9-10 (MSG)

3. Are you willing to allow God to use your story to bring life to others?

"Jesus said, 'Go home to your own people. Tell them your
story, what the Master did, how He had mercy on you.'
The man went back and began to preach in the
Ten Towns area about what Jesus had done for him.
He was the talk of the town."
Mark 5:18-20 (MSG)

"Choose to not live in woe is me.
Choose to live in WOW is me!" Holly Dowling

Fighting Time & Finding Purpose

Don't Whine—Win!

Kathy Walters Burnsed

THERE IS
ALWAYS

HOPE

Kathy Walters Burnsed greeted me at her front door with an enormous smile and a laugh that made me feel at home even before I'd crossed the threshold. Tea and cookies sat waiting on a tray in her beautifully decorated home, and I could hardly wait for her to share her story with me. From what I could see, it looked sure to be one of fairytale perfection. She laughed as she admitted her husband lovingly refers to her as "the bluebird of happiness," but, oh my, has God been gracious to her.

• • •

I was the reigning Queen of Frantic. My to-do list was impressive, and I usually completed most of it each day. All around me, I'd hear comments like, "Wow! What a fireball! How does she do it? Work, entertaining, and taking care of others! What a superwoman!" Little did everyone know how the treadmill of my life was rapidly increasing in speed, and I was struggling to keep up.

My main problem was I felt incapable of saying "no" to any opportunity that came my way. I could see something fun and joyous in every task I was asked to do, whether it was ministry events, social outings, or friendly entertaining. No matter the task or time it required, I was there and loving it. I was very good at saying, "yes," but never realized the danger of being spread so thin.

I took pride in the fact that the tasks I agreed to do were "good." Oh, how subtly Satan worked to deceive me. He knew I wouldn't participate in something if it were inherently evil, but that is his way of operating in a believer's life. The enemy was sly and cunning as he led me to believe that saying "no" to ministry or doing something nice for somebody else, was a sin. After all, "They NEED you. YOU are so good and kind; no one else could get the job done as well as you."

My life changed in the blink of an eye when we moved our family to Tennessee. I was forced to leave my comfort zone, and go to a strange city. Thus began one of the loneliest times of my life. I started to whine and asked God, "Why have you put me here?" It felt as if I'd been placed in a never-ending "time out" as some punishment for a sin I could not remember committing. It was as if God had said, "Go sit in that old chair and don't move until I say you can." Trust me, for this hyperactive, social butterfly, my timeout felt like the worst thing in the world!

But God, in His incredible wisdom and generosity, knew I needed the opportunity to reconnect with my husband, my children, and myself. He knew I needed to slow down and learn to say that magical word— "no." God knew the deepest desires of my heart even when I had forgotten them. He gave me the time and resources to acquire my heart's desire long before I ever thought to reach for my dreams myself.

The day after we moved, my children looked at me and asked, "Mom, when are you going to take us to daycare?" It broke my heart, as daycare was all they'd ever known. I was the last mom to pick her children up each day, but I told myself it was alright because I was working really hard with church ministry.

What began as an opportunity to slow down quickly faded. I returned to what was most familiar and once again began saying "yes" to everything. I was steadily increasing my speed of life to accomplish it all. I never stopped long enough to question myself or to notice the impact my hectic days were having on my family.

Each Wednesday night, I'd pick the children up, and we would rush to prayer meeting, often not returning home until after ten o'clock at night. I knew I was tired, and I could only imagine how worn out their little bodies were. It wasn't long before we were all sleep deprived and burnt out.

I wish I had seen those three years as the precious gift God intended it to be. Instead, it felt like all I ever said was, "Can we hurry up and get going?" I spent my days complaining and whining, yet God still continued with me, wanting me to learn precious lessons on how to live for Him. He said, "Kathy, even though you don't recognize what I'm doing, I'm pouring extravagant generosity on you. Even though you don't see it as such, one day, you will." In the gentleness of His love, He gave me time to learn and to grow.

After three years, we returned to Savannah and life was very different for a while. I started working at the local arts school, and my career path wasn't as frantic as before. I was able to enjoy the same vacation times the children had. Working for the school system was God's gift of giving me quality time with my kids. We were blessed and able to travel, doing all the fun things God lined up.

But slowly, once again, I turned the speed up on my activities. I wanted to be like a saltshaker, shaking God's salt all over the world. God opened some of the most amazing doors in municipal government, pharmaceuticals, and other career paths I would have never considered. One of the most important lessons I ever learned was: "God doesn't call the qualified; He qualifies the called." God is generous. I continue to marvel at how He created us and what great things He can do with beings so small.

On one particular day, I was sitting at the airport in Chicago on my way to a business meeting when I began to watch people—really watch them. I was struck by how quickly they all seemed to be running. I'd never really noticed it before. They were almost frantic and chaotic. They were each participating in my best event: the never-ending dash. As I looked at them through spiritual eyes, all I could see was emptiness. It was a very powerful revelation. It all appeared so very sad. I had to ask myself, "At the end of the day, does it really matter?" The more I thought about my pace and lack of balance in life, all I could say was, "Lord, I'm just tired."

The recession hit shortly after my revelation that I was too busy. The economic climate resulted in thousands of layoffs across the country. I was retrenched. It seemed God had placed me in another "time out," and I had still not learned to appreciate it.

"God," I whined, "did You just put me on the shelf again?" With my work experience, skills, and connections, everyone said, "You'll find another job in no time, Kathy."

But, I didn't.

I've since learned it doesn't matter what we know or how well we know it. What matters is *Who* we know, and the connections *He* lines up for us. I realized in hindsight that the Lord gave me this second "time out" to prepare my heart. Time is all any of us have, and it is fleeting.

Sitting at home with 40 plus extra hours every week left me wondering what I was supposed to do. I remembered that day at the airport as I watched the frantic people rushing past, and I started to write. From the depth and quiet of those long moments, my book, *Perfect Timing*, was born.

Though I have not always recognized it, God's generous, abundant gift to me has been those "time outs," which turned into pivotal points in my life. I learned to slow down the treadmill, be quiet in God's presence, and I found out I could be comfortable in a place of quality, fruitfulness, and beauty.

Trust me, just like a little child I still have moments where I struggle to see that "time out" is not a punishment, but a gift. I now can see God set me aside during each of those down times. He took me out of the limelight and into a place of seclusion. It was what He did with Elijah when He took him to the brook, Cherith. God provided for Elijah's needs, but not necessarily his wants. My quiet years were painful, and I often filled them with complaining. But even through my complaining, God managed to use the time to draw me closer to my husband, my children, and Himself. If I'd kept doing the dash, rushing frantically from one activity to another, I would have lost everything I held dear.

I'm so thankful that every time I started to complain about a time out, the Lord said, "Complain all you like, little missy. I want you to learn to enjoy this time." Once I was able to grasp the concept and begin to understand the purpose of the times of isolation, I realized quiet time was all about developing my relationship with God.

Life was never intended to be about how much I could cram onto my to-do list and into my day. It has always been about God, and how I can best use the gift of time, which He provides each day. I am finally learning when to say "no" to fast-paced busyness. This single lesson, which has taken me so long to learn, has forever altered the direction of my life.

I now start each day praying Psalm 90:12. "Lord, teach me to use wisely all the time I have." What a different prayer from all the years I prayed, "Lord, can we get this show on the road?" I no longer become panic stricken when opportunities disappear behind closed doors. I am learning to wait on God and rely on His perfect timing.

In being totally transparent, I want you to know there is still so much more I need to learn. There is a higher level of trust I need to attain, and a deeper level of confidence I'm reaching for, but I can taste it now!

I am so thankful that during the "time outs" in my life, God provided for my needs. He sent me manna each day and listened to my wailing and complaining. Did He take care of all my wants? Thankfully, no— because my wants are seldom what I need.

I now choose to place myself in "time out" whenever I sense an attitude of whining and complaining about to begin. As I wait on God in my self-declared state of isolation, I ready my heart to receive another extravagant gift of renewal and grace that He is waiting to pour generously from His hand.

• • •

For more about *Kathy Walters Burnsed* and her book, *Beating the Clock: Managing Time God's Way*, visit PerfectTimingToday.com.

Invite Kathy to inspire and train your team. She combines inspiration, motivation, and humor that delights both large and small audiences.

For Prayerful Application

1. Has there been a time in your life when all you have seen are the pieces that are missing? Does this lead to endless complaining? Words have power and impact not only our attitude but also the lives of everyone around us.

> *"Death and life are in the power of the tongue:*
> *and they that love it shall eat the fruit thereof."*
> Proverbs 18:21 (KJV)

2. Have you included God in the details of your daily life? Please meditate on this verse when returning to time management God's way.

> *"Teach us to number our days,*
> *that we may gain a heart of wisdom."*
> Psalm 90:12 (NIV)

3. Can you see God's protection and provision in your "time-out" experiences? For further study, read how God took care of Elijah during the drought of his life in *1 Kings 17*.

> *"If I really want an unrushed life,*
> *I must underwhelm my schedule*
> *so God has room to overwhelm my soul."*
> Lysa Terkeurst

Driven, Duped & Delivered

Don't Whine—Win!

Juliet Van Heerden

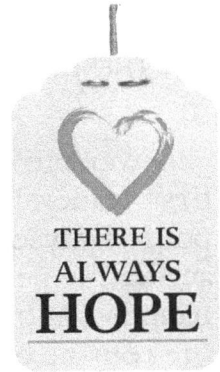

THERE IS
ALWAYS
HOPE

We had a few, fun-filled hours doing a photo shoot. Juliet had me sit at the base of a huge oak, on a stump at the beach, playfully posing in the old ruins of the island. Her thorough, meticulous passion for all of her work reflected in every shot. When we both became too hot and tired, we flopped into comfy chairs on the deck of the little Bistro at the Jekyll Island Hotel in Georgia. We munched on our lunch and sipped delightful Southern tea. Before I knew it, I was entranced by her story.

This beautiful, tall, young woman was born in Missouri and moved with her newly-wed parents to Arkansas where they lived for five years until her mom and dad divorced. That is when Juliet, her baby sister, and mom moved to Texas to begin a new life. She has no memory of life when her parents were together, so her happiest childhood moments were spending long, Arkansas summers with her grandmother and great grandmother. She felt at home with them.

Childhood wasn't entirely carefree for her, but she found enjoyment in school and solace in reading. She loved being outside, and climbing trees. Her mother remarried when she was seven and suffered through another divorce seven years later, which was the catalyst for their move to Pennsylvania where her mother tried to escape the pain and begin again.

• • •

I went to a Christian boarding school and held my first leadership position with the student council. I poured myself into sports. My inner drive fought for academic perfection, but I still made time for the friends I adored, and I always had a boyfriend. I liked the routine of my life, and always having a guy around made me feel safe.

After graduating, I studied elementary education at Southern Adventist University and followed my love of learning and my dream of becoming a teacher. Once again, I had a new boyfriend. I thought we might get married after I graduated. During that time, my mother became engaged to a kind man in Switzerland. She and my 16-year-old sister planned to move there after an August wedding just before my senior year at the University.

Around that time, an unfortunate incident put a damper on all of my plans. I fell off of a barn roof during my summer job as a painter, breaking my back and hip. The doctor ordered me to stay put and not even go back to the University for my senior year. I felt fine and didn't listen, so I attended my mother's wedding and proceeded on to a hard year at school, determined to graduate on time.

I wasn't able to sit still for very long because of the steel rods along my spine, so I would stand in the back of the classroom for lectures. I healed slowly, despite my refusal to rest properly. That painful experience of being physically broken changed the dynamics in my relationship with my boyfriend. After graduation, I had to have another surgery to my spine. Although he was there after the surgery, I felt he viewed me in a different way.

I noticed he never spoke about marriage or commitment anymore and I could only infer that it must be because I was broken and damaged now. I hid my emotional hurt from him and everyone. Against doctor's orders, I interviewed for teaching positions and received an invitation to teach in Washington D.C.

As I began setting up my classroom, I felt overwhelmed and as if I couldn't handle teaching. That feeling was the first indication that my injury did not affect my physical well-being alone; something happened to damage me emotionally. I quit the position before I even started, and went to visit my family in Switzerland to try and work out my emotions.

While in Switzerland, I was in a car accident with my mom where I re-broke my hips. My mom was severely injured as well, suffering brain and spinal damage along with a shattered arm. We ended up in the hospital together for six weeks. My new stepdad was our nurse.

I fought depression and felt myself entering its dark cavern. A friend sent me the book, 7 Habits of Highly Effective People, and I felt inspired reading it. I continued to strive for perfection through my rehabilitation, though my body and mind felt shattered. My college boyfriend came to get me once I was allowed to leave the hospital. He took me back to the States.

What an awkward time it was, being a "drifter." I had no home, no job, and nowhere I felt comfortable. Those safe, happy summers at Mamaw's were long gone. All my things were in storage as I stayed with my boyfriend's parents in Missouri for a while. It was hard to stay faithful to the rehab exercises required for my recovery. I didn't feel very attractive, and my boyfriend began to feel more like a brother. He left me to stay with his parents after he accepted a position as a bird guide in Costa Rica. I felt stuck.

A few weeks later, he called and invited me to come to Costa Rica to work as a supervisor in the lodge kitchen. He thought the tropical sunshine might help me to heal. The warmth beckoned me, so I accepted his offer. He treated me as one of the guests at the lodge, and our relationship quickly fell apart.

After I broke up with my boyfriend, the lodge owner's son showed interest in me and was emotionally attentive, so I transitioned my affections to him. At the time, I couldn't see what a poor choice I had made.

I slowly recovered from my injuries and decided to go back to the States to begin working as a teacher. My biological father had a vacant apartment in Tulsa, Oklahoma, which I temporarily moved into. My new boyfriend followed me to the States and stayed with his sister in Dallas. It felt good to be pursued, and I justified staying with him despite all of our differences.

Until now, all of my boyfriends were of my same religion, but this one wasn't and had habits I was unaccustomed to. I didn't know to ask questions about his past with drugs or alcohol or any previous marriage. I accepted everything at face value and ended up blindsided due to my lack of wisdom.

I began a job at a small school where I was the only teacher for all grades. Wanting to be successful, I worked extremely hard, but the job only lasted one school year. Christmas day brought a proposal and a ring from my boyfriend, and we planned a Costa Rican wedding. I was twenty-four when we moved back and married on the beach. On our honeymoon, I realized I had made a big mistake, but I said nothing and pretended to be happy living with my choices.

The next two years revealed my husband's hidden habits and lifestyle. Smoking and alcohol had been part of his life since age six. I didn't realize it, but he was also a drug addict. I buried the pain of each unpleasant discovery in busyness. I loved working at the lodge, birding, and the Costa Rican culture. I started a ministry by selling souvenirs and trinkets to tourists and used the money to buy rice and beans to share with the impoverished natives. My work was fulfilling, but my marriage was not.

I couldn't identify exactly what the problem was; it was as if my husband had a separate life, apart from me. Exhausted by attempting to unearth aspects of him he was fighting to keep hidden, I focused my time and effort elsewhere and learned to find joy in different ways. That is when I discovered the art of being still with God, both in nature and in giving.

After two years of living at the nature lodge and working for my new in-laws, I felt we needed our space. We moved back to the States where I found a teaching job in Central Texas. A school board member offered my husband a construction job. He took the job and joined my church, giving me hope that we could make the marriage work. We made Christian friends, and I honestly thought life was better. I tried to ignore the little things that still didn't add up.

My sister went through a divorce after a sad, 18-month façade, and asked if she could come live with us. The three of us decided to start a coffee shop and café. We collectively invested all we had.

I became the baker, shopkeeper, and cleaner-upper, in addition to my day job as a teacher. My sister was the barista, sandwich maker, and host. My husband was the accountant. The business was very successful in that we served great coffee, soup, and food and were voted the best café in the area for our first two years. Strangely, we struggled financially.

We discovered, much too late, that my husband started using cocaine again. To support his habit, he regularly altered the books and stole cash. I was devastated and completely unprepared to deal with the truth. What a complicated, difficult, and awkward time.

"I'll quit. I'm sorry. I'll never do it again," became his often repeated promise. I became increasingly frustrated with the repetition. His addiction became so bad, his health collapsed. He realized his choices narrowed down to the final ultimatums: rehab or death.

I dropped him off at rehab and cried the whole way home. "God, how are you going to fix this?" I felt I no longer had a marriage and had transformed from a wife into a babysitter and watchdog. I wanted my husband to become well and I desired relief from the weight his sickness placed squarely on my shoulders.

After rehab, we began seeing a Christian counselor who worked with addicts. My husband remained clean for almost a year. During that time, my hope for recovery and restoration rose, though I continued to struggle to keep my teaching career, business, and marriage afloat. Around this time, my sister became engaged and moved away, so we closed the café. My husband and I started building our home, and I began dreaming of becoming a mom.

A few months later, a friend called asking if I would foster a newborn baby whose mom had been on crack cocaine. I went to see the little girl and instantly fell in love with her. The baby also found a place in my husband's heart, and he agreed to participate in a foster-to-adopt program, with the intention of keeping her forever.

We started all the mandatory parenting classes and completed our paperwork. "Our" little girl would visit every day. I picked her up in the afternoons after school, played with her, bathed her, and then took her home to bed. We had a very sweet bond. The day came when our little girl would come home to stay.

Our social worker had one question. "Have you ever been in a drug rehab program? We don't see it in your paperwork." We had left out that detail, but somehow they found out the truth. Her next sentence has haunted me for years. She became very somber and said, "You were dishonest on your paperwork, which is against our policy. I'm sorry, but that disqualifies you from our program."

I was devastated. They came and took our little girl, which sent my husband into a spiral of addiction that was so long and dark it almost killed him. For him to survive, he needed to leave the area. There were too many triggers where we were at, so we sold our dream home and moved.

We both found new jobs, made a few friends, and led a simple life in a new place. We were messed up financially, and it wasn't long before my husband started using again and ended up back in rehab. This time, he was kicked out for breaking the rules and went straight back to using. I didn't know what to do.

Mechanically, I'd go to work and do my job while I silently begged God for an escape from my situation. I didn't want to walk in my family's footsteps of divorce. I sometimes wished my husband would just die so I could be free. We went to church every week, and my husband served as a deacon. I couldn't stand him living a double life.

I told my family bits and pieces of my pain, but I didn't speak freely about the roller coaster cycle of rehab and relapse. I thought I was protecting them from continually having to forgive him as I did. I thought I was protecting him from shame. Eventually, he started disappearing for days, coming home defeated, dehydrated, and super skinny. I'd nurse him back to health, wondering if even jail could help him at this point.

I suspected he was dealing drugs on top of his addiction and could only speculate on the details of his life I was ignorant to. I could feel the darkness coming into our home when he'd sneak in. Regardless of those awful nights, I pretended to be strong and happy each morning for my first-grade students. I began to feel more and more scared and started sleeping at a girlfriend's house at night to avoid my husband or involvement in any of his illegal shenanigans. Soon, I was staying at her place several days at a time.

I unexpectedly decided to go home one afternoon, and discovered another woman's underwear in my laundry room. Infidelity never crossed my mind before that moment. I knew my husband loved drugs more than he loved me, but I never dreamed another woman was involved with my husband.

I was so angry and hurt upon discovering a new level of betrayal. I confronted him, and my husband declared he no longer wanted to be married to me. After almost 13 years of fighting tooth and nail to avoid it, our marriage ended in my worst nightmare, divorce.

The following summer, my mom and I went on a mission trip to work with refugees in Italy. Through blogging about my experiences, God began to reveal to me how much He loves each of us as individuals. I realized as my marriage became worse and worse, my relationship with God had become better and better. God was the One who never lied to me, and the only One I could trust. I learned how to forgive and to live in forgiveness.

I began to see every person has a story, and to seek out each one's testimony, not focusing on the surface level circumstances. The young refugees on Italy's streets shared their stories with me and broke my heart. My eyes opened to the suffering all around the world that far exceeded my own. God gave me compassion for others who were hurting. What a summer! God did a lot of healing work in my life through that missions trip.

Following my glorious Italian experience, the enemy sent a snare into my life in the form of a man. As my custom was, I took the bait and toyed with the relationship for months. I was so accustomed to always having a man in my life; it was hard to be alone. I enjoyed the positive attention and longed for a decent relationship. The man wanted marriage right away.

I found myself asking, "Lord, is this relationship from You?" He answered through the counsel of godly friends who were not afraid to speak the truth in love. The answer was not what I wanted to hear, and I did not want to heed their advice. In God's infinite mercy, He granted me the strength to walk away and was spared from making another huge mistake.

It was painful to let go of the relationship. I put my heart out again for the first time, and I felt defeated by the outcome. I asked the Lord to open doors for me to move me out of that town. I needed a new beginning and a place where I could become the woman God wanted me to be. I prayed, and God opened the door for me to go back to Southern Adventist University to pursue my Master's degree.

I arrived on the familiar campus and said, "Lord, I left here fifteen years ago with nothing. I'm back with nothing. I am fully Yours. I would like to have a godly husband, but it's up to You to find him for me. I choose to stop being co-dependent with men and only to be dependent upon You."

Pursuing my Master's degree turned out to be less about furthering my education and more about experiencing a journey of learning to depend on God.

It was hard to resist returning to the familiarity of belonging to someone out of fear or loneliness. I had to learn to stop trying to control my destiny through my work ethic, drive, and current boyfriend. I had to step out on faith and trust God to catch me. I'm happy to report He hasn't failed me yet. After going through Christian counseling for a while, I realized how easy it was for me to see the addiction and problems my ex had, but it was tough for me to identify and take accountability for my issues. I needed healing.

After a few months of returning to school, God provided me with a beautiful Cape Cod-style home in Georgia, a teaching job I loved, and the opportunity to complete my Master's in Literacy, which was a lifelong dream.

Then, the Lord brought André into my life. This time, I was cautious and wise about guarding my heart. I had a sense of calm and peace in my spirit, believing God was in charge of whatever happened. I didn't use my old tricks to woo or chase, but backed away and let God and André do all the work.

God used those years to grow me up and teach me how to learn to love and trust a man who was also growing in grace. We became engaged in 2009 while in Italy visiting my family. We were crazy about each other and had developed a committed, godly relationship. I knew I didn't need to fear a marriage with André. I finally allowed God to be Captain at the helm of my life's ship.

I've now been married for six years to that good, godly man and I know what pure love is. I know what it means to have a mature, emotional relationship with a husband. The brokenness of my home life as a young person inflicted me with an unhealthy insecurity that manifested itself in control and a co-dependent pattern of seeking love. As a result, my life carried a theme of self-reliance and repeated loss. But, through the healing that came with complete surrender to our loving, Heavenly Father, I discovered a new theme for my life: *God redeems the things we thought were lost.*

P.S. God also gave us two teenage, orphaned Ukrainian sons! How God orchestrated that is another story!

• • •

Juliet's speaking truly impacts the hearts of women. If you would like to invite her to speak to your group or to order her memoir, *Same Dress, Different Day*, you can do so at:

www.JulietVanHeerden.com.

You can read the journey of finding and adopting her sons on her blog and Facebook page at:

www.facebook.com/juliet.vanheerden

"When one door of happiness closes, another opens, but often we look so long at the closed door that we do not see the one that has been opened for us."
Helen Keller

For Prayerful Application

1. Have you suffered physically or emotionally because of poor choices? No life is perfect, but our attitude toward ourselves, others, and God can make a huge difference in the way we handle our imperfect worlds. We are called to live blameless lives and to speak words that uplift others, even in the midst of our personal issues. Think about how can you apply the following scripture to your situation.

"In everything you do, stay away from complaining and arguing, so that no one can speak a word of blame against you. You are to live clean, innocent lives as children of God in a dark world full of crooked and perverse people. Let your lives shine brightly before them."
Philippians 2:14-15 (NLT)

2. Perhaps you love someone who suffers from addiction. Maybe you are the addicted one. It's natural to point out other's flaws while ignoring ours. It is not until we look closely at ourselves that we realize those around us are not the only ones with issues. When we can face our personal trials truthfully, believing God is refining us through every step, we can find joy, even in the most difficult of journeys. In what ways have you found God's joy today?

"My brethren, count it all joy when you fall into various trials, knowing that the testing of your faith produces patience. But let patience have its perfect work, that you may be perfect and complete, lacking nothing." James 1:2-4 (NKJV)

*"Dear brothers and sisters, whenever trouble comes your way,
let it be an opportunity for joy. For when your faith is tested,
your endurance has a chance to grow. So let it grow, for
when your endurance is fully developed, you will be strong in
character and ready for anything."*
James 1:2-4 (NLT)

3. When God began to redeem the things I thought were lost, I vowed to live in the present and to not shackle myself to the past by always complaining about it to people around me. Are you hurting the ears of those who listen to you by spewing negativity? Would those who are closest to you be able to say that your words impart grace and encouragement to them? Prayerfully listen to your speech as you move through the day.

*"Don't use foul or abusive language.
Let everything you say be good and helpful so that your words
will be an encouragement to those who hear them."*
Ephesians 4:29 (NLT)

*"Let no corrupt word proceed out of your mouth,
but what is good for necessary edification,
that it may impart grace to the hearers."*
Ephesians 4:29 (NKJV)

AFFIRMATIONS, THANKSGIVING & PRAISE

Know Your Strengths,
How God Created You,
Be Thankful, Sing Praises.

Affirmations, Thanksgiving & Praise

Know your strengths, how God created you, be thankful, sing praises.

THERE IS
ALWAYS
HOPE

"I praise You because I am fearfully and wonderfully made;
Your works are wonderful, I know that full well."
Psalm 139:14 (NIV)

Do you believe that you are wonderful? Beautiful? Strong? Courageous? Do you believe you matter? That each part of your story matters? Do you know it full well?

For each of us, there are seasons when we do not believe each of these aspects. We all have little stories within our big story that challenge our strengths and plunge us into our weaknesses. We're human, born into our imperfect families in a turbulent world, yet the fact remains—you are beautiful!

God uniquely designed you for a purpose-filled life. If you do not believe that, it's time to discover it. Find your strengths, your gifts, and core values. Understand your needs, goals, and dreams.

If you do not find your purpose, you easily plunge into attempting to meet the needs, goals, and dreams of others. If you do not find your purpose, you will give into an unhealthy way of life that ultimately leaves you dry and empty. You end up hurting the very people you serve and love, which crushes you to the core.

Be aware of your weaknesses as they facilitate how and why you make the choices you do. Knowing your weaknesses will enable you to make wiser choices.

Affirm yourself daily by writing down at least three positive aspects of yourself. It can be as simple as, "I smiled at a stranger today," or "I didn't yell at my kids." Perhaps it's, "I do have a beautiful smile," or, "I have such a healthy head of hair." Every day, notice what makes you uniquely you. If you cannot see the good in yourself, seek help. Take that bold step to start the process.

You truly cannot have peace or deep inner joy if you do not treasure yourself and know your value. Your view of others and how they treat you will change as you love and respect yourself. You will be empowered to make healthy and wise choices.

A key to accessing the wonder of affirmation is to transition each affirmation into thanksgiving, and, ultimately, praise to God. When you state your affirmation, thank God for that unique aspect of yourself. Tell Him He's incredible for designing you so intricately. Something miraculous happens to your soul when you begin to thank God on a real level for who He made you to be. God's light enters as you allow Him in, and your heavy burdens are lifted away.

"Let them give thanks to the Lord for His unfailing love
and His wonderful deeds for mankind,
for He satisfies the thirsty and
fills the hungry with good things."
Psalm 107:8-9 (NIV)

"Gratitude unlocks the fullness of life.
It turns what we have into enough, and more.
It turns denial into acceptance,
Chaos into order,
Confusion into clarity.
It can turn a meal into a feast,
A house into a home,
A stranger into a friend."

Melody Beattie
Co-Dependent No More

He Knows Your Name

Affirmations, Thanksgiving & Praise

Linda Znachko

I was about to sip on my morning cup of tea in the hotel restaurant when my eyes focused on the elegant lady walking toward me. I smiled and asked her to join me. Before long, she started sharing what she does. My heart paused. I was enthralled and deeply moved by her love for God. I could barely wait to hear more. In the few years that followed, we have become friends, worked on our books, and have seen what God does when we say yes to Him.

God used Linda to unlock the secret, unmourned grief of my mother's death, which I had held in my heart for 20 years. Together we said goodbye to my mom as we watched rose petals drift into ocean waves. Linda's words and prayer facilitated a space for God to heal me. I am one of the many she purposefully serves.

• • •

My life radically changed the summer of 2009. It began innocently enough as I opened the paper one morning to read the news, and a local story drew me in. Someone found a baby amongst the trash in a city dumpster, abandoned and dead.

The reporter referred to her as Baby Doe and wrote that the child was naked except for a diaper. I read the story with growing horror as I pictured her tiny body, cold and alone, in a filthy dumpster. It was more than I could bear, someone throwing their child away with yesterday's garbage.

Through my growing outrage, I felt God brand a message into my heart. It's a message that continues to burn within me and has defined the purpose of my life.

A dumpster is not a grave.
A diaper is not a burial robe.
And Doe is not a name.

How could I just close the paper and pretend I'd never read the story? I felt compelled to respond. Even though Baby Doe had already died, I felt impressed she still needed a safe family, a family who would name her, and mourn her death. She needed a family who would remember she was once here, even for a brief moment.

As I closed the paper down on the table, I sensed God speaking to me once more. "This one is yours, Linda. Pick up the phone and call."

I found the name of the reporter and made the call. On his advice, I contacted the coroner. Little did I realize it would be the first of hundreds of similar calls.

"You're the only one who's called," he told me.

We spoke for a few minutes, and then he said, "We will probably bury this baby in a mass grave."

"A marked grave?" I asked.

"No, just a mass grave."

Seriously? I thought.

"This is so unacceptable to me," I responded. "Will you please list me as a resource to ensure this child is given a name and buried with dignity?"

The months slipped by. A criminal investigation opened and slowly inched its way through the judicial system. I wrote letters and called the coroner every week. I had no knowledge of the law, no experience with legal proceedings, but the Lord showed me what to do at each step.

As I continued to call week after week, relationships began to grow, and doors started to open. Opportunities to speak and minister began to pour in. By the time the case officially closed, 13 months later, God led me to start a new ministry called *He Knows Your Name*. In the years since, the Lord has continued to show me the best way to teach others how to honor and bring dignity to their loved ones who have died.

To walk in a sacred place with a family as they grieve the loss of a child, which is surely one of life's deepest heartaches, is such a powerful experience. Each time, I am drawn into their fold of grief as they desperately seek for hope. In those moments, I show them the love of Jesus. It is the best gift I can give and the one they need most. My faith strengthens as I speak of Jesus. It is incredible to watch His love heal and transform wounded grieving hearts.

Later, someone sent me a story from Wisconsin about a 14-year-old rape victim who delivered a stillborn baby. Someone gave her a grave for her baby, but she didn't have a headstone. When the man who'd assaulted her was finally found guilty and sentenced to jail, a kindly sergeant told her he hoped she would now find peace.

She tearfully whispered, "I still don't have a headstone for my baby."

Moved with compassion, the sergeant placed an ad in the paper to help raise funds for a headstone for her baby. I went to see the girl and had the privilege of sharing the story of Jesus with her. As I told her how much Jesus loved her and wanted a relationship with her, she exclaimed, "That's just what I've wanted—a relationship!" We purchased her baby's headstone and had a graveside burial.

We live in a culture of fear when it comes to grieving and death, in spite of the fact it is something we all understand. We have all experienced our share of brokenness. Life brings both joy and sorrow, yet God shows us that through it all, we can have hope. We can experience joy in life again. Because of Jesus, I no longer fear death.

As I work with people stuck at the crossroads of desperation and hopelessness, I encourage them to stand up and walk. I share the truth that Jesus stands outside of the tomb. I speak light into their darkness and gentle whispers of life anew. Through His love and promises, I tell them they will make it through their time of oppressive darkness.

I invite them to let Jesus walk with them, and assure them even though they feel as they too have died, God can resurrect them in spite of grief. They can expect to live joyfully once more. God still has so much planned for them.

People crave to live in the light. They just need someone to show them how. It is important we don't become stuck in our grief. Even when we don't know the reason why, we can—and must—move beyond asking "*Why?*" We may never find the answer to our "*Why?*" Instead, we need to ask, "*What now?*"

Over the years, the *He Knows Your Name* ministry has expanded and grown to include more than abandoned babies. I have also been able to help indigent families who are unable to purchase headstones. As I meet the families, I share Jesus and offer them hope. I love to watch as they find healing in honoring their loved ones with dignity, and begin to find closure. The following story is one of many that illustrates the healing work God does.

The media snatched up the story of the 13-year-old boy who died in a pool accident. They were quick to demonize the mother, portraying her as negligent, and the child as a bad kid. I met with the mother, and as I came to know the family, I realized how inaccurately the media had reported their story.

I worked with the mother for a year. I mentored her and taught her about Jesus. She stopped using abusive substances and made healthy, life-changing choices that effectively turned her life around. We then started a foundation to fund water safety and swimming lessons for children in their poverty-stricken neighborhood.

Something positive came about because of that young boy's life. A plaque with his picture now stands in the local park. Children who participated in the program run up to the boy's mother and proudly tell her that they can now swim. Life and hope resurrected in her because she is now a steward of her son's legacy.

Too many women wander around not knowing God's purpose for their life. The Lord knows I've done my share of wandering. Through it all, I've learned we don't have to spend the rest of our lives wondering what we were born to do. Jesus says, "I have come that they might have life—more abundantly!" It is a promise and can become your reality. He wants to give you life, abundant life, today.

Something incredible happens once we accept the gift of life Jesus offers. We become life-givers. When we share the gospel of Jesus, we plant seeds of love and hope into lives that have grown numb with pain. The abundant life He gives us flows through us and into the lives of desperate and dying people.

God is calling women everywhere to embrace their purpose and become life-givers. Realize God has crafted you with unique abilities to share the abundant life that flows from His heart of love. Daughters of the King are called to be life-givers, and so we can change the world. Each one of us brings life in a unique way, empowered by the Holy Spirit.

So how do we discover the way God has called us to be life-givers? Don't be surprised or afraid if He takes you down a difficult road to show you the way. Shortly before that morning in October when a news story helped define my life purpose, my mother died after an 18-month struggle with cancer. In my season of brokenness, God birthed an opportunity to help others, and I said "yes."

My mother entrusted her funeral arrangements to me. I helped pick her burial clothes and helped my dad choose her headstone. In everything I did for her, I felt privileged to honor her and give her dignity. It was an incredible, life-giving experience for me. In the sacred moments of deepest suffering, I learned death provides an opportunity for God's light to shine in the darkest of times.

Along with my mother, I have also lost a brother and a sister-in-law to cancer. I have learned not to fear suffering and death, for I have profoundly experienced the sweet presence of Jesus in those moments. I believe He reserves a sweet chalice of grace to drink from in the deepest, darkest time when we wrestle with death. In grieving death, we taste and see God in new ways. As I walked with Jesus through mourning my mother, Jesus built into my heart a treasure of gold, refined in the fire of suffering. He gave me a glimpse of Himself and the promise of renewed life.

Looking back, I can see the lessons I learned from my mother's death profoundly impacted the way I responded to the news of Baby Doe. I clearly understood the importance of bringing dignity to the dying, of honoring them, of respecting their life and the memories we have of them. Though I didn't realize it at the time, God was preparing me for the work He was about to call me to do.

God's mercies are new every morning. Revelation 21:5 says, "He who sits on the throne is making everything new." God regenerates everything, breathing life for the purpose of multiplication. Even through death, God desires to bring life. He calls us to die to ourselves every day then fills us to overflow with His abundant life. He gives us words of love and seeds of hope to plant in hurting hearts, which restore life and joy. He calls us to be life-givers like He is, a restorer of the broken.

He calls you Daughter. He knows your name. You are a life-giver.

• • •

Linda is the founder of *He Knows Your Name*, a ministry that gives children a name in life, and dignity and honor in death. Linda also partners with mothers who do not want their children's legacies to be the circumstances of their death. Her aim is to assist the grieving to find healing through loss and to find purpose in knowing every life is sacred to God.

Linda is a sought-after speaker for churches, conferences, and retreats. She has discipled women for over 25 years. Over the last six years, local and regional media regularly interviews her.

She is married to Steve, and together they founded the *Zacchaeus Foundation*, which funds ministries across the globe. They are also dedicated advocates of *Safe Families for Children of Indiana*, the state where they raised their four children and currently reside.

For more about Linda or to purchase her book, *He Knows Your Name: How One Abandoned Baby Inspired Me to Say Yes to God*, visit: www.HeKnowsYourName.org.

For Prayerful Application

Read Luke 10: 25-37. The passage is full of questions that need to be answered with an honest and teachable heart.

1. Who is my neighbor?

2. Am I most like the priest, Levite, or the Samaritan?

3. Who have I radically loved that best represents the Samaritan in this story?

4. What stirs you to show compassion for someone? Is it a visible bruise, mental illness, or beaten up emotionally broken heart?

5. How has a stranger ever loved you at high cost? Write that person a letter of gratitude and take action by "paying it forward" and loving someone else.

Every time a vulnerable life is honored,
other unlikely lives are touched.
Linda Znachko

The Knife &
The Knowledge
Affirmations, Thanksgiving & Praise

Rachael Hartman

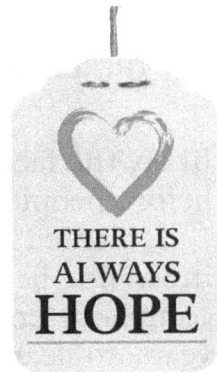

THERE IS
ALWAYS
HOPE

She quietly slipped into the room at one of my monthly gatherings. I could tell from her eyes that crowds weren't her favorite, yet there was courage and grit. We have spent many precious moments together since that day, sharing our love of tea, purpose, and Jesus.

Rachael published my book, Your Story Matters. It has been a gift for me to step into her story, understand her boldness, and the fiery passion her crown of red hair hints at.

• • •

We were a military family; Dad was an Army Chaplain. I was self-conscious and felt I was different because I lived with an unspoken list of expected standards for a "preacher's daughter."

The constant moving every couple of years, sometimes every six months, amplified my shy personality. I'm 33 and have lived in over 30 houses. All of the transition added grief to my struggle to make friends. I always felt like an outsider.

I was bullied and experienced social rejection in junior high and high school, which led to a problem with self-destructive, implosive anger. I felt like there was something wrong with me, and that must be why I struggled to make friends. In reality, it was more likely the fact that I was new and reserved, and moved before people had the opportunity to get to know me.

I blamed myself for their "rejection," thinking I must not be good enough to have friends. I would complain, engaging in negative self-talk. It took me years to learn how to accept a compliment. I also struggled with Body Dimorphic Disorder; all I could see looking in the mirror was a big nose.

The one thing I did love about myself was my hair. I received many verbal affirmations for my red hair. "Words of Affirmation" is one of my key love languages, so words matter a lot to me. Unfortunately, negative words are also powerful to me, and destructive to my heart.

When I was ten, someone said I was "chunky," so I started limiting my eating. I became very conscious about what I ate, mentally beating myself up for eating unhealthy foods. At 15, I began fiercely exercising and began to move into exercise bulimia. I'd eat what I wanted and then workout to purge. My social anxiety increased as I sought perfection and tried to please people.

When I was 16, I encountered an opportunity with my dad's friend, a plastic surgeon, who offered to "fix" my nose, if that's what I wanted. It was a free offer, and I thought I would have more friends if I was prettier.

I prayed and fasted, asking God if it was "okay" to have plastic surgery. I had peace about it, so I decided to go forward with the rhinoplasty and chin augmentation. I had no idea how the operation would impact me or who I would become afterward.

There was a component of plastic surgery I hadn't anticipated—the immense physical pain and recovery. I stayed home for weeks dealing with the after-care. It took an entire year for all the swelling to go down. I was still developing and growing as a teenager and had to grow into my face. I felt numbness in my lips and feared it would never go away.

After the surgery, the main thing I realized was that I hadn't changed as a person and that the inside of me had nothing to do with the outside. Plastic surgery didn't change my problems, even though the experience launched me in the right direction. After the surgery and my epiphany that I was still "just me," I began to move forward doing the hard work necessary to develop my character.

Thankfully, I can say I don't regret my choice to go forward with the surgery because of all I learned from it.

I knew I had to start working on my self-esteem, social skills, and combating anxiety. I didn't know how to be my own best friend, so I had to learn. I didn't know how to allow myself just to be who I was without trying to force my personality or body into a societal mold I accepted as "the best." I had to learn to be kind and to love myself.

The surgery took up a few months of my focus, but life did begin to move forward. We moved from Georgia to North Carolina. I entered my senior year of high school, started to drive, and worked a part-time job. I increased my prayer life, made a best friend, and started dating. Good things were happening, but my inner experience of the world did not change overnight.

Mine was a quiet journey of healing and growth. People who knew about my experience with cosmetic surgery advised me not to talk about it, even though I longed to. They said people—especially church people—would judge me over the decision. I became even more fearful of social rejection. I felt insecure. I kept my choice private, as it was no one's business anyway. Inside, I was still very vulnerable and longed for healing, for someone to understand.

Twelve years later, I began talking publicly about my surgery for the first time. Soon after that, God led me to begin writing a book to share my life lessons with other people. I wrote about what I wish I knew before my surgery, and all I learned through prayer and introspection after the experience. My book is titled *Facing Myself: An Introspective Look at Cosmetic Surgery.*

I have finally come to a place of contentment and acceptance of both my body and my personality. It has taken a lot of work, counseling, reading books, as well as digging deep into my family history and the generational beliefs passed down to me. It has been a process, and a journey to come to a place of not making decisions to please others. Only the power of the Holy Spirit has given me the ability to step out of a materialistic spirit that left me feeling unworthy and unloved.

I now understand it is a lie to believe risking life to make a cosmetic change will transform a person into someone beautiful or desirable. God has brought me into a community of people I need to be with; people who encourage, uplift, and accept me for who I am—

even with my flaws and imperfections. God is my source of peace, fulfillment, and joy. He is my Creator, and I know I am "fearfully and wonderfully made."

I had to learn who I was in God's sight and begin to shift my focus on pleasing Him. I had to identify sources of negativity in my life and shut down those voices, whether internal or external. As I've deepened my relationship with Jesus, I am learning to see myself as He sees me, slowly but surely.

I talk to many people, both women and men, who are considering cosmetic surgery. Our culture attaches a lot of shame to our bodies. Often, cosmetic surgeons base their marketing schemes on our vulnerabilities. *"Find the new you. Create yourself to be who you always wanted to be. Younger. Newer. Perfection."*

But changing the body can only bring temporary happiness, and a distraction. The knowledge of going "under the knife" changes life, but not always in the way we think it will.

I've pondered the spiritual significance of my cosmetic choices. I've asked myself the question: What am I giving my body, time, blood, and money to?

I must hold myself accountable for my mental and spiritual health. I must make well-informed decisions, and realize that the experiences I go through will change my life. I want my choices to bring me closer to Jesus. Only a relationship with Jesus, daily communicating with Him through prayer and His Word, can bring wholeness and completeness.

• • •

To connect with Rachael, or to learn about her publishing business, visit www.OurWrittenLives.com.

Rachael is the author of two books: *Facing Myself, An Introspective Look at Cosmetic Surgery* and *Called to Write, Chosen to Publish, 20 Inspirational Thoughts for Christian Writers.*

She has written two other books for hire as a ghost writer, and has worked with over 30 authors to publish their books.

"The beauty of a woman is not in a facial mode,
but the true beauty in a woman is reflected in her soul.
It is the caring that she lovingly gives, and the passion she
shows. The beauty of a woman grows with the passing years."
Audrey Hepburn

For Prayerful Application

1. Is there anything you feel you must do to be beautiful, perfect, or to receive God's love?

> *"God saved you by his grace when you believed.*
> *And you can't take credit for this; it is a gift from God.*
> *Salvation is not a reward for the good things we have done,*
> *so none of us can boast about it."*
> Ephesians 2:8-9 (NLT)

2. How do you deal with inner conflicts and desires you know may have negative consequences?

> *"So I say, let the Holy Spirit guide your lives.*
> *Then you won't be doing what your sinful nature craves. . . .*
> *Those who belong to Christ Jesus have nailed the passions*
> *and desires of their sinful nature to His cross and crucified*
> *them there. Since we are living by the Spirit, let us follow the*
> *Spirit's leading in every part of our lives."*
> Galatians 5:16-18, 22-25 (AMP)

3. Do you practice people pleasing or are you focused on a relationship with Christ?

> *"Trust in the Lord with all your heart,*
> *do not depend on your own understanding."*
> Proverbs 3:5 (NLT)

Rising to Royalty
Affirmations, Thanksgiving, & Praise

Angelena Cortello

THERE IS
ALWAYS
HOPE

I gently lay her book down, better understanding the process and lifestyle of addiction that had entered my life through a family member a few years ago. Hope filled my heart, knowing that God can heal and change everything. A few weeks later, our tea time was over the phone. Angel's solid strength, wisdom, and profound understanding of how God works took me to His throne room.

• • •

I do not hide behind my childhood experiences, as we all need to take responsibility for our choices and actions in life. Yes, I had a typically dysfunctional home filled with issues, family problems, and a lot of emotional and verbal abuse in my early years. Add to that, I had bipolar disorder which went undiagnosed until I was sixteen. I also had obsessive-compulsive disorder, another piece of the mystery to why I didn't function well.

My troubles worsened in my teen years. As depression increased, I'd overeat and take as many diet pills as I possibly could to lose weight. A negative turning point happened at school as I watched friends coming into class laughing. They were tripping on

LSD, but all I saw were happy people, and I wanted to be happy and smile like they were.

I didn't know their happiness was counterfeit, or that the experience would leave me feeling even worse when it was gone. Once the effects of the drugs wore off, I would feel so guilty I would use again to numb the guilt.

I also had a lot of relationship issues. I didn't know what a healthy relationship was supposed to be. When I met a guy, I did whatever I could to keep him in my life, thinking I wasn't worthy of him. I took people-pleasing to a whole new level. He was my world, and I did whatever he wanted, losing myself in him.

We smoked weed together, and through our "open relationship" he introduced me to prostitution so I could make money for us. My extreme efforts to please him ran him off, and our toxic relationship ended when he broke up with me on Christmas Eve.

The breakup was hard on me. I felt lost and rejected with no identity. I was devastated. I lost my "clients," as they were his friends, which left me with no income and no drugs. I had no idea how to rebuild my life without him in it.

I got in my car and drove aimlessly. I pulled in at a gas station and saw a man sitting on a curb. I could tell he was an addict.

"If you can take me to where I can find some dope or drugs, I will take care of you," I said.

He took me to a crack house filled with men. I didn't know any of them. Still distraught over my breakup, I smoked $400 worth of crack that night, not thinking I could become addicted. I thought I could manage my drug use, but the drugs ended up managing me. I remember walking away feeling dirty, ashamed, embarrassed, and trashy.

I continued to seek out my addiction. I met a woman in a crack house who was well put together. She looked at me and said, "Hey kid, what are you doing? Do you work?"

I told her about my part-time job, and she and the others laughed at me.

"No, do you work?" She asked again.

Finally, I figured out she meant prostitution. She promised me I could "work," make unending money, and smoke all I wanted to. The men in the room begged me not to go, but she reassured me she takes care of her girls.

She introduced me to her many clients, as she was well-known in Miami. There was no need for me to stand on corners hustling for tricks. Her dad was her greatest enabler. He was a retired cop who molested her all of her life. He would get her out of any trouble she found herself in.

She had us, her small group of girls, and we had a place to live and an endless client base. As the youngest of all of the girls, I was the favorite for some time, until another young girl came into the picture. Depending on each man's various preferences, he would pick out one of us to become his regular girl. The system worked because they offered us drugs until we were totally addicted; then we were at their mercy. We would do whatever they wanted. It's an illegal business, but that's how it works.

Somehow, through it all, I developed keen street smarts when it came to discerning people's intentions. I attended church for three years as a young child, and I knew the Holy Spirit had marked me. Many times, I would be in a motel room or crack house and men could see I didn't fit in. They would even comment on it.

God made Himself very real to me, even in my active addiction, by wanting my attention and holding onto me.

I moved between jail and rehab multiple times. Before my last court date, before moving to Louisiana, I looked at a room full of women addicts and prostitutes.

I asked them, "What are you going to do to make money when you get old? How do you get a job without a resume when all you've done is work the streets?"

They all became quiet. It was a turning point for me.

"Oh, dear, this is going to be me," I thought to myself. God whispered again to me, and I knew the street life was not His will for me. I remembered I had promised Him as a child that I would one day sing in the church choir. The seeds of faith were planted deep within me and kept pulling at me. There was more to life than the life I was living, and I knew it.

Still, I did not believe in myself or that I could change and be clean and sober. On my last court date, I said to the judge, "Please don't spend your tax money on me and another rehab. Let me just do my time and let me do what I know how to do. I'll be back on the streets."

The judge said, "Look at all the people that have been addicted for years. You are still young enough to have an opportunity to change your life."

My family asked the judge to move me back to Louisiana. He agreed. "I will give you the best of both worlds, and send you to Louisiana to complete your probation and rehab there."

There was a war inside of me between my spiritual side and my addictive side. On the plane to Louisiana, I said to God, "If you can help me get off crack, I will sing in the choir and give my life to You and do the best I can."

I bargained with God as if I were talking to a dealer. I knew no other way to talk to Him. Instantly, I felt something slam shut in me. I knew in my spirit the life I led was over and my life would be completely different, though I had no idea how it would happen.

Once I arrived in Louisiana, I went to church and was re-baptized. This time, it was my decision. It was my way of saying to God, "I want you to lead my life. Wash my past and history clean."

I started over with God's hand on my life and went to church and counseling. I took medication for bipolar disorder, attended 12 Step meetings, and did whatever I was told to do. I was desperate to be different from the girl I had been.

After attending church for six months and listening to the choir sing, I heard in my spirit, "*Something is going to happen. Your life is going to change.*"

I had no idea what was going to change, but I believed it had something to do with drugs and my history of chronic relapse. At the time, I was going to a rehab program at the Salvation Army. I had to suddenly swap programs because that one wasn't state-approved as the judge's order required.

My Uncle helped me get into a 30-day residential program, but I was angry. I was stuck in a house and couldn't join the choir. After arriving at the program, they tested me for all kinds of diseases. I was tested many times before in other rehabs and was always disease-free.

The test results came back on April Fools Day, and I found out I had Hepatitis B and HIV. At the time, I wasn't upset because I believed God would heal me, now that I was committed to Him. I told myself I would have the elders of the church lay hands on me, and pray for me, and all would be good.

I started HIV treatment, which seemed to be working well, but the virus wasn't going away. It was hard for me to accept what I had done to myself, and how much my choices had destroyed the body God gave me.

I started teaching Bible studies, and volunteering at prison ministries, trying to prove my love for God through what I was doing. Maybe, if I worked for Him, He would heal me. There was much turmoil in my head, as I tried to figure out why God wasn't blessing me as I thought He should.

I soon realized everyone wanted the same thing in life—healing for themselves—and I was no different. Why cards unfold the way they do, I don't understand. I learned I could get bitter and angry, or accept it.

Five years later, I was still not at a place of acceptance. I was highly involved in living for Christ and making a difference, but I was becoming angrier by the day and intensely bitter. One day, I went to a Louisiana bayou and had it out with God.

I vented and lamented. I thought I shouldn't have to suffer the consequences of my choices. I complained that the plan I had wasn't happening as I thought it should. Where was the white picket fence with the family, success, and the perfect life?

He said, *"You noticed I didn't do it all? So, whose will are you living in when I choose to say no? You say you want My will, but if you really did want it, you would accept it when I decide to say no."*

I was at a crossroad. I had been clean and sober for five years. I could leave that bayou, reject God, and live how I wanted to, or I could accept His will and continue what seemed to be the path where all my dreams were crushed.

Would I still be a Christian? It is easy to live for God when everything works out, but what do you do when everything doesn't work out? I had to think about it and make a choice. Did I really want God in my life?

I stood up and proclaimed, "I don't always agree with Your will or how things have unfolded, but I have lived without You, and I don't want to live without You again."

I submitted to making His dreams come true instead of chasing my dreams. That day was the day of my actual conversion. Once I had been through the valley and faced real challenges of life, I was ready to choose Him fully, for real.

I had to answer the question: Can I live for God on a bad day? I choose to live for Him, no matter what, even on the bad days. Even when I don't get my way, I choose Jesus.

At rehab, the counselors and other professionals told me I had a self-esteem problem. They were right. If I loved myself the way God wanted me to love myself, I would not settle for abuse, be it emotional, physical, or sexual.

If I loved myself, I would never have put a substance into my body to destroy it, whether drugs, alcohol, tobacco, or unhealthy food.

If I loved myself the way God loved me, I would not ever be in a toxic relationship that has the potential to destroy my destiny.

I have learned I am royalty. I am His child. I deserve the best life God has for me, and so do you.

• • •

Angel lives in Louisiana where she is pursuing a degree in a medical field. She treasures each moment she is alive and believes life is meant to be fun and enjoyable.

Her life revolves around God and making a difference in the world around her. She spends her time mentoring women in recovery from addictions and speaks at churches and recovery events.

To invite Angel to speak or to buy her books, *Angel, the True Story of an Underserved Chance* and *Healing Letters, a 140-Day Journey of Healthy Living*, email her at angelenacortello@bellsouth.net.

For Prayerful Application

1. Do you own that you a child of the King of the Universe?

"So in Christ Jesus you are all children of God through faith."
Galatians 3:26 (NIV)

2. Can you protect your body, heart, and soul and guard yourself as a treasure?

"Put to death, therefore, whatever in you is earthly: fornication, impurity, passion, evil desire, and greed. These are the ways you once followed, when you were living that life. But now you must get rid of such things—anger, wrath, malice, slander and abusive language from your mouth. Do not lie to one another, seeing that you have stripped off the old practices and have clothed yourselves with the new self, which is being renewed in knowledge according to the image of its Creator."
Colossians 4:5, 7–10 (NRSV)

3. Do you choose to live in the fullness of Christ today with thanksgiving?

"As you therefore have received Christ Jesus the Lord, continue to live your lives in Him, rooted and built up in Him and established in the faith, just as you were taught, abounding in thanksgiving."
Colossians 2:6 (NRSV)

"God wants us unstuck and experiencing peace with our past, purpose in our present, and passion for our future."
Pat Layton

ESSENTIAL LIFE SKILL 3

LIVING A HEALTHY LIFESTYLE

Mentally, Emotionally, Spiritually & Physically

Living a Healthy Lifestyle

Mentally, Emotionally, Spiritually & Physically

THERE IS
ALWAYS
HOPE

A healthy lifestyle encompasses the mental, emotional, spiritual, and physical part of our beings. The first two skills profoundly impact every unseen aspect of our lives, as well as the physical condition of our bodies. Likewise, each skill impacts every aspect of our lives. Our physical health makes a difference in our spirituality and emotional and mental states.

It is important for us to keep an awareness of how we are doing in each area of our lives. We must follow up regular self-assessments with action steps to correct any area that is out of balance.

As you practice the daily art of not complaining, assess your decision-making skills. Are you making good decisions? Plan positive action steps that lead to your goals. Believe you are beautiful and empowered for greatness. Every day, decide and believe you will move toward your goal. Set yourself up for successful living.

Our attitudes and beliefs are powerful. Many scientific studies prove how our attitude impacts our health and vice versa. An added strength of embodying a positive attitude is having a physically strong and healthy body. I encourage you to research the power of thought. Once again, the Bible has wisdom to share:

"Do you not know that your bodies are temples of the Holy Spirit, Who is in you, whom you have received from God? You are not your own; you were bought at a price. Therefore honor God with your bodies."
1 Corinthians 6:19, 20 (NIV)

As with all God's laws, they benefit us! He made us and knows what works best. His law is not just for survival, but is given to us so that we can live life to the fullest!

"The thief comes only to steal and kill and to destroy; I have come that they may have life, and have it to the full."
John 10:10 (NIV)

So, let us choose a good attitude and view taking care of our bodies as a joy! It takes discipline to care consistently for our physical bodies. Too often we think of discipline as a burden, or as negative. Let's re-frame discipline to be a gift!

As we form new habits, we will be equipped to progress. Research to find what is best for your body and circumstance; choose to put into practice what is required. Believe you can, and commit to action and repetition.

Repetition. Repetition. Repetition.

Do not give up. Find an accountability partner or group. Set SMART Goals (see the Appendix for more on SMART Goals). The key to success lies in asking the

Lord into the journey with you. He will show you your weaknesses and how to rise above them.

You will discover how your unmet needs, hurts, and inner voices, or the voices of others, impact your struggle with diet and exercise. Use affirmation, thanksgiving, praise, and careful monitoring of your words and thoughts. Repeat scriptures that empower you with strength and courage.

To reinforce the joy of healthy living and the required building blocks, I'd like to introduce you to the word JABULA. Jabula is an isi-Zulu African word that means, "To Be Happy."

"JABULA" Building Blocks for a Happy, Balanced Life

J - Joyful eating: Choose a healthy diet
A - Activity: Engage in adequate exercise
B - Balance: Plan for good rest
U - Up There: Get out in the sunshine and fresh air
L - Laughter: Make time for fun in your life
A - Attitude: Continue in thankfulness

Choosing to take care of your physical body is one of the greatest gifts you can give yourself. It reveals how much you truly value who God created you to be. Discipline challenges us to search deep within for self-revelation.

We find ourselves asking many questions. *Why do I struggle with self-control? Why do I choose the things I do? Do I respect myself enough to care for my body?*

Our answers often reflect the value we put on ourselves. Your body is the only vehicle you have, and it will either deplete or energize you.

In Christ, you can treasure this gift of life and care for the body He gave you.

"Pay mind to your own life, your own health, and wholeness. A bleeding heart is of no help to anyone if it bleeds to death."
Frederick Buechner

Voice, Advocate, Protector

Living a Healthy Lifestyle

Courtney Santana

THERE IS
ALWAYS
HOPE

Courtney rocked the room as she took the stage at EBW 2020's weekend retreat. We danced the night away with gusto as her soul-filled, rich, heart-wrenching voice compelled a response from everyone in the room. Yet, when she speaks, her gentle, quiet voice masks her tenacity, fervor, and story. She is a force to be reckoned with and a joy to know.

• • •

Constant longing for my absent father affected my self-confidence and decisions about a life partner. I became a people pleaser. To keep people in my life, I'd do whatever made them happy, with no regard as to how it affected me.

My loneliness led me to cling to an abusive relationship during the time I was pregnant with my daughter. I convinced myself the man wouldn't harm her. I couldn't bear the thought of my daughter being fatherless and suffering fear of rejection and abandonment as I had.

The relationship began with verbal abuse. He would call me names, control me, and isolate me from friends and family to the point where I even lost jobs. Physical abuse followed, which left me with a broken eye socket, broken ribs, and a miscarriage during my second trimester.

The abuse continued for four years.

Inevitably, his life choices led him to jail for six months. While there, he wrote letters to reconcile, promising to fix his behavior. He said he found religion and was in Bible study.

Longing to keep a father figure for my children, I believed the Cinderella story. I took him back and believed the whole situation would be redeemed. The cycle of him crying and me taking him back continued several times. Each time, I was always praying, "God, please save my family."

Then one day, I prayed a different prayer. "God, Your will be done. I don't know what the future will look like. I'm sacred. What now?"

Of course, the abusive man said the right things during his next visit after being released from jail. He sat on the couch, took his coat off and went to the restroom. I prayed my new prayer.

As he was in the bathroom, I picked up his coat, and a gun fell out. It was a God moment. I would later discover another God intervention that day in the fact that I parked my car outside. I always keep my car in the garage. My son was a happy baby and never made a noise, yet, that day, he screamed and yelled as he sat on the couch. It gave us a little moment, some camouflage, to escape. We fled to a shelter where, thankfully, they had room for us. We stayed for three months.

Friends went to check on the house for me and found it trashed, holes shot through walls and mirrors, windows broken. It was clear God was shouting, confirming that if I had stayed, it could have been the children and me who were hurt or killed. It was as if God was saying, "It's not about your wants and desires; think of your kids."

I was thankful to be alive. At first, I was miserable, crying, and rude to people. I felt I didn't deserve what was happening. It was inconvenient. I was better than all of this. God's inner voice became louder as He spoke to me. "You need to pull yourself together." I started seeing His grace is new every day.

Starting my life over had to be a permanent transition. I had to make the decision to let go of trying to keep my children's relationship with their father. Perhaps it would work in the future, but not at that time. Thankfully, I had supportive friends and family who watched the game play out.

Fearful of what would happen when we left the shelter I began making a plan to move away under protective orders. Time would be the best way to heal. I had to have no contact with him. He knew what to say and how to keep me in his grasp.

Love is a powerful thing. Words are powerful. For that man, our relationship was not about love; it was about controlling me by saying everything I wanted to hear. Time away gave me the opportunity to start changing the dynamics of our relationship and finding people to pray for my healing.

Even though the relationship between us was over, I blindly stepped into other abusive relationships in friendships and at work. Then, once again, I found what I thought was love. I wanted a healthy, nonabusive marriage, so I married the new man. We were not ready for a proper marriage. He was ill-equipped to cope with me; I turned a blind eye to a lot of things, and the relationship fell apart.

After that, a controlling friend started in on my life. She would call and email all day. She consistently showed up, highly upset with other people in my life. I began to experience the same physiological reactions I had with my abusive exes and realized I hadn't healed.

I made a choice to move away. I finally learned I needed time for spiritual healing within, not just removal from a person. Understanding the process of emotional healing compelled me to write my book.

I thank God for the journey now, as it gives me perspective and understanding as to why I made certain choices. I am so very thankful that I'm able to make better choices, living entirely in my gifts, and able to make a difference in the world.

One of my gifts is music, which has always been part of my life. I used to dance for a dance company which morphed into me playing the flute. I sang while attending the University of Texas, was involved with theater groups, acting in musicals and plays. I also had my own band for 20 years. Now, I'm writing my music and working on a CD. It began when I was living in the shelter, where I wrote between 150 and 200 songs.

Later, I would I serve on the board of directors for the very shelter I had once fled to. In 2011, I founded *Survive2Thrive Foundation.*

I started speaking, sharing, and researching why so many survivors, both men, and women, say they couldn't get into shelters. I discovered the problem was survivors were not rehabilitated enough by the time they left, which lead to a staleness in the shelters as the same survivors kept coming back. There was no room for new survivors.

Typically, survivors don't know where they will go after living in a shelter. I realized they need to change their internal beliefs about being a victim. They need help with their mindset once they escaped their traumatic experiences.

Altering patterns of thought requires work to change and reprogram the brain. I decided to create the tools to give and empower these brave survivors to succeed and to move forward in life. I wanted them to believe "God and I do this together" and not only rely on others to help them through life.

I am now married to Gary Santana who supports my foundation and is about to start a program for men called, *"The Purple Bowtie Movement."* He will work with people who are abusive, and who have experienced abuse themselves. Gary is also my "Roady" music manager. My daughter helps us with events and fundraisers, as does my son who is handy with power tools! We all believe in fortifying others and lifting them up where light and HOPE can touch them. God tells us to be an example, shine a light, and allow Him to take us to a place where He can speak through us. He does the rest.

People won't experience judgment from me. I give everyone as much grace as God gave me. We cannot judge others; we don't know where they have been. Look at me; I came from hiding in a closet to meeting the President of the United States. Yes, I did!

I was lobbying for a domestic violence hotline at a press conference and met the Vice President who was sitting next to me and the Mayor of Austin. He asked if I would come to Washington to talk to the Deputy Director. I arrived in DC and learned the visit was moved to the following day. Unfortunately, I wasn't able to stay. When I told them of my conflicting schedule, they told me to go to 1600 Pennsylvania Avenue—the White House!

While at my meeting with the Deputy Director, President Obama walked by and started chatting with me! I don't think I heard half of what he said. At that moment, I was so thankful God had taken me from such a low-low place in life to standing there in the White House, sharing my message.

The purpose of *Survive 2 Thrive Foundation* is to transition survivors of domestic violence from victimization to empowerment, and the next level of success. They are called to thrive, whether in finishing their GED at age 40, starting an entrepreneurial pursuit, or journeying to healing. **Abuse is no longer an option.** We are no longer victims.

It is essential to give victims the tools they need to reach success and to teach them how to use those tools. We must use self-awareness to protect and take care of our physical bodies, heal emotionally, and understand spiritual wholeness. We must empower each person to climb the next mountain or face the next challenge.

Survive 2 Thrive Foundation has a goal to be a national entity within five years. We are building an e-care box, a recovery program, and developing advocates and mentors who have already finished the program to work with new survivors as they begin their journey.

• • •

Not only has Courtney learned to have healthy relationships, she now takes better care of herself, has lost 145 pounds, and glows with health!

To connect with Courtney and to learn more about her work, visit www.Survive2Thrivefoundation.org.

For Prayerful Application

1. Do you allow another person to hurt you physically, whether it be a slight smack, slap, punch, push, a shove, or throwing you, beating you, or locking you up? It is not OK.

"But understand this, that in the last days there will come times of difficulty. For people will be lovers of self, lovers of money, proud, arrogant, abusive, disobedient to their parents, ungrateful, unholy, heartless, unappeasable, slanderous, without self-control, brutal, not loving good, treacherous, reckless, swollen with conceit, lovers of pleasure rather than lovers of God, having the appearance of godliness, but denying its power. Avoid such people."
2 Timothy 3:1-5 (ESV)

2. Do you allow others to abuse you verbally or emotionally? Do you allow others to put you down, yell at you, tell you you're a failure or belittle your dreams?

"Who is wise and understanding among you? By his good conduct let him show his works in the meekness of wisdom. But if you have bitter jealousy and selfish ambition in your hearts, do not boast and be false to the truth. This is not the wisdom that comes down from above but is earthly, unspiritual, demonic. For where jealousy and selfish ambition exist, there will be disorder and every vile practice. But the wisdom from above is first pure, then peaceable, gentle, open to reason, full of mercy and good fruits, impartial & sincere."
James 3:13-17 (ESV)

"There are six things that the LORD *hates, seven that are an abomination to him: haughty eyes, a lying tongue, and hands that shed innocent blood, a heart that devises wicked plans, feet that make haste to run to evil, a false witness who breathes out lies, and one who sows discord among brothers."*
Proverbs 6:16-19 (ESV)

3. Can you declare that your body is God's gift for you to treasure, and create boundaries to protect it? Will you protect your body from sexual abuse in any form by anyone?

"Do not give dogs what is holy, and do not throw your pearls before pigs, lest they trample them underfoot and turn to attack you."
Matthew 7:6 (ESV)

"The most common way people give up their power is by thinking they don't have any."

Pulitzer Prize Winner Alice Walker
The Color Purple

The Unexpected Stroke

Living a Healthy Lifestyle

Karen Pearson

THERE IS
ALWAYS
HOPE

With eager anticipation, I stepped into the room where I knew I would meet her—the woman who had married Michael, my long-lost friend from college days. I knew Karen had to be a special lady if he had chosen her. Looking back, I believe I met Michael for the gift of sisterhood that Karen and I would find in each other.

It didn't take long for us to bond deeply. A ministry for women developed as we shared life and our deep love for Jesus. We have walked far and learned much. Together and apart, we have laughed and cried over countless cups of tea and stories of God's incredible love for us and others.

Now, decades later, I still see her as I did at our first encounter: beautiful inside and out. Gentle, kind, giving, creative, and smart with a resolute determination and strength. Her love for Jesus is the center from which her life pivots. She is one gifted lady, and I am blessed to call her my friend.

• • •

I grew up in Zimbabwe and was only fifteen when I met Michael. He was from South Africa, had recently graduated from college there, and was working as a professor at a college just outside the city I was living in. We met at church and started dating.

When the war forced the college to close, he was asked to serve as a church pastor, and has been in the ministry ever since. Shortly after I turned 18 and finished high school, we married.

Michael was working as a pastor in charge of a large district in one of the most dangerous parts of the country. It was hard work, and life drove us to our knees daily. We were so very aware of how much our lives and ministry depended on God's providence and grace.

Just as the country had grown war-weary, my heart was weary too. Though I was young, my many life experiences led me to early maturity, which happens with heartache.

When I was a little girl, my grandmother lived with us. She was a blessing, but her struggle with mental illness impacted us all. My 15-year-old uncle lived with us too, and as a scarred young man, his choices brought devastation to my little-girl heart that remained hidden for decades.

I learned there was safety in silence, so I didn't share my pain with anyone; however, the emotional damage didn't go away. Because time doesn't heal all wounds, my inner strength and resilience gradually eroded. I believed terrible things about myself and, eventually, the weight of all my inner pain began to impact my health.

Michael, being older, could see my weariness and continually brought our situation before the Lord. Michael has loved me at my best and my worst, even when my worst was ugly. I knew God had brought this gracious man to me, and I trusted God more than I trusted my own hurting heart. My heart was conflicted and afraid, so unsure of who I was, what it meant to be married, and how to be a good pastor's wife. There were days when it all felt so overwhelming.

What a miracle that our God never lets us go. His love holds us close, always. In my fragility, I often lived off of spiritual crumbs from the Lord's table, yet as I followed Him, He led me to the feast He had prepared for me.

Chronic stress ultimately weakened my immune system and robbed me of courage and perseverance. For years, I would become ill, suffer migraines, and literally pass out. I lived in a fog of fearfulness and depression. I regularly spent days where I would go through the motions of living—all the while, feeling completely disconnected. I was barely surviving.

But God held, sustained, and taught me through His Word. In Lamentations 3:22-23 (NASB), the prophet Jeremiah said, "The steadfast love of The Lord never ceases, His mercies never come to an end, they are new every morning." God is faithful. The sweetest stories in life are the ones where we find joy on the other side of pain. God brought His healing to my broken heart and taught me how to receive the unfailing love of my sweet husband.

My confidence grew through love from Michael and Jesus. I knew I had to step out in obedience to get help for my body. I chose to learn how to live a healthy lifestyle and what a journey that has been!

I received quite a bit of help from my body, which became violently ill at times and pushed me to seek for answers and pursue health. My headaches became progressively worse, knocking me out for days and leaving me exceptionally weak. I sought dietary help, combined with alternative medicine, and a slew of tests revealed severe allergies to dairy, soy, gluten, and duck.

Duck? Really? I never ate that in any form. For the most part, I was a vegetarian. But duck and goose feathers in my pillows and comforters triggered painful migraines, and still do. Removing them from our home and requesting an allergy-free room when traveling has made all the difference.

It's not easy to stick with radical changes in lifestyle and diet. Sometimes all I want is chocolate, ice-cream, and comfort food.

But when I indulge, there is always a price to pay. I now read labels carefully, make my food from scratch, and have learned to be creative. I lost sixty pounds during the process of pursuing health. I always try to be prepared and have food on hand that I can eat without becoming sick. Physically, I cannot afford to let my guard down.

Exercise has also become a regular part of my life, and so has adequate rest—another immense challenge. As a perfectionist, I push myself so hard, and I've had to learn that there are lines I must draw when enough is enough and the day is done. Finally, I began to level off and live in my "balanced and healthy normal." I experienced new energy and wellness like never before. I even added regular massages and visits to the chiropractor to my regime.

While at work about six months ago, I suddenly felt awful. Something was terribly wrong. I called Michael to come and take me home. As we were leaving, a co-worker told Michael to take me to the ER. He did. Soon after arriving at the hospital, I became unresponsive and could feel myself slipping away. The doctors set to work, and once they had me stabilized, they sent me by ambulance to the main hospital in town. It turned out I had a stroke.

How on earth was that even possible, given my diet and lifestyle? After subsequent testing, they discovered I'd experienced a tear in the vertebral artery. A small part of the artery wall had sheared off, and a small blood clot had formed underneath it. When the clot ultimately came into my brain, the stroke occurred. My neurologist said he sees four or five cases like mine each year. It's a miracle that no paralysis occurred.

I had to take long-term sick leave from work to have time to rest and reflect. Coming that close to death has a way of realigning perspectives! I'm so grateful for the chance I've had to re-evaluate what matters to me. It's changed how I approach everything in life. I've been able to separate from work at the end of each day—and leave it at work.

I rejoice in the love Michael and I share together. He can still make me laugh faster than anyone I know. My writing and speaking ministry has become more sharply defined, and there is a Divine urgency to be obedient to all God calls me to do.

My passion and purpose is to share the story of God's incredible love for us, and the news of His soon return. We are all dealing with the things of eternity, and yet how easy it is to overlook reality. Life is not only about feeling better on this side of Heaven. Jesus calls us to go into the highways and hedges, and bring others to the wedding feast. He asks that we give of ourselves, telling others of our experiences of His healing. When we do, they can see His character in us, and gain hope, courage, strength, and life through our stories.

How can I not give my life and stories to the Lord? For He has turned my tears to laughter, my pain to peace, and my weakness to strength. He is my joyful story. Please let Him be yours.

• • •

Karen lives in Nampa, Idaho, where she serves as director of publicity and public relations at Pacific Press® Publishing Association. She is an author, speaker, editor and avid storyteller. One of her greatest joys is to work with authors, helping them develop their skills and craft their stories.

To connect with Karen, visit www.karenjpearson.com, or email her at Karen.Pearson3@gmail.com

For Prayerful Application

1. Do you accept you are God's child? Will you choose Jesus today, to be your go-to King, Father, Savior, Friend, and Love?

"In Christ Jesus you are all children of God, through faith."
Galatians 3:26 (NIV)

"But to all who received Him, who believed in His name, He gave power to become children of God."
John1:12 (NASB)

2. Do you believe that even when you are experiencing dark times wrapped in a thick cloud, God can use it for good? Can you believe that when things seem to be against you, you can trust in the God who is for you?

"And we know that God causes all things to work together for good to those who love God, to those who are called according to His purpose . . . If God is for us, who is against us? He who did not spare His own Son, but delivered Him up for us all, how will He not also with Him freely give us all things?"
Romans 8:28, 31-32 (NASB)

"Dear brothers and sisters, when troubles of any kind come your way, consider it an opportunity for great joy. For you know that when your faith is tested, your endurance has a chance to grow."
James 1:2-3, (NLT)

3. Will you turn from harmful choices, take the challenge, choose Him, allow Him to change your life and live in His joy daily?

*"Repent and be baptized, every one of you,
in the name of Jesus Christ for the forgiveness of your sins.
And you will receive the gift of the Holy Spirit."*
Acts 2:38 (NIV)

*"But a full life doesn't mean an easy life.
In many cases, it means just the opposite."*
Michele Cushatt

From Savor to Savior

Living a Healthy Lifestyle

Cathy Rodgers

THERE IS
ALWAYS
HOPE

I briefly met Cathy when I spoke at a business mixer and was touched when she supported my very first event held in Savannah. Shortly after that, I received a call from her where she promptly stated how marvelous it all was, but that I missed the point. Point being that to make a difference in the lives of women, they need to hear about Jesus.

"Welcome to the South," I thought. I had not shared Jesus. I did mention I believed in God, but I was a humanist at that time. Later that year, my dad died, and God brought me back to Himself. After many months, I heard what Cathy had said. We spoke about her comment, and she shared how embarrassed she felt, as it was not like her to say things like that.

In the years that have followed, we have become good friends—growing in Jesus, building businesses and choosing to live a healthy lifestyle. Her story is one that shows God off in a big way, and what happens when He steps in.

• • •

I was a Florida girl who lived a few years in Japan during my dad's civilian contract working for the military. As a child, I distinctly remember my classic after-school snacks were syrup sandwiches, or marshmallows smashed into a sandwich bag, then squeezed into my mouth through a hole torn in the corner of the bag. Healthy living was not part of my life, not that Mom didn't diet—she was always on one. We kept cottage cheese, Fresca, and milk of magnesia in our fridge.

I met Jesus at a youth retreat when I was about 13-years-old. For two and a half years, I learned life lessons in church that made a huge impact on me. God gracefully provided that haven for me during those years, as my parents were on the verge of divorce.

The changes in my family facilitated an early start in the working world for me. I found a job at Disney while in high school, and it was easy for me to drift away from God. I found the love and attention I needed in a boyfriend. I was earning an income, and feeling quite independent.

I married at eighteen, and two years later I had my daughter. Four years later, I was a divorced, single mom. Despite the fact I had a baby, I made a way to go to college and still work in the party lifestyle.

I was soon involved with another man whom I also married. He kept up the appearance of being a godly man but was far from it. Dark times followed for my daughter and me, and only years later did I understand some of the things that had transpired. He and I finally divorced.

That is when I started dabbling in new-age books. One thing led to another, and I bought into many different philosophies, including karma. God was quietly stirring, holding His hand over me and even using my wayward experience to build an appreciation in me for depth in relationship with Him, compared to the emptiness without Him.

The deeper I dug into new-age thought, the more I noticed the philosophies justified bad behavior and lack of responsibility, even the murderous act of abortion. One day, I finally said to myself, "This just doesn't make any sense!"

Slowly but surely, I started turning back to the truth of Jesus. I met Bill, who at first thought I was crazy with all my weird books and beliefs. Once we decided to marry we wanted to join a church, as we were raising teenagers together.

I discovered Joyce Meyer on TV and began listening to her CD's and tapes. Her ministry began a process of de-programming my mind and healing the emotional damage leftover from divorces and bad relationships.

I had to learn how to deal with my regrets and the choices I had made, which impacted my daughter. Slowly, I began to understand the truth and walk through the complicated process of self-forgiveness. I became very focused and passionate about the Word of God. As God healed me emotionally and spiritually, I began seeing myself through His eyes. Then he moved me to the next step—physical healing.

Just like my Mom, I was a yo-yo dieter my entire adult life. Sadly, I never learned how to nourish my body. I had a wake-up call when I could no longer diet myself back into my favorite Saint Patrick's Day pants. A few weeks later, I was invited to photograph a diabetes fundraiser walk and decided to have my blood pressure checked at one of the booths. My numbers were sky high, but I knew I never wanted to take medicine for it. The final straw came when I saw pictures of myself from that day. I declared, "I need to do something!"

If you had met me during that time, you might have thought I appeared quite normal. But there were silent health concerns going on with me. I had already had my gallbladder removed, and was diagnosed with pre-diabetes, high cholesterol, digestive issues, and high blood pressure. I took sinus medicine and antibiotics year round and was out of breath when I bent over to tie my shoes. I ate and drank whatever I wanted to, not ever thinking about consequences.

I just 'happened' to run into a friend who had lost some weight and asked her what she had done. She referred me to her health coach. I soon took the leap, went on a five-day detox, and lost six pounds! I was shocked, as I lost more than just water weight. The program was not a fad diet, and it seemed manageable.

I began learning more about health and nutrition and stuck with a group of like-minded women who inspired me and held me accountable. I kept going, and within a year I lost about forty pounds and my blood pressure went down! I also went on a supplement regimen, which eliminated the sinus infections I had every time the season changed. Looking back, I believe I could have saved my organs, even avoiding a hysterectomy, had I led a healthier lifestyle.

The process of losing weight was not easy. I journaled how I felt every day, along with what I ate, drank, and the exercises I did. I added scriptures and read them aloud daily to help me through the process of change. These steps led to a journey with God, a time of healing and growing. I had to learn to be self-disciplined and to find my strength from Jesus daily, sometimes hourly. I started understanding what it meant that we only have one body, and how neglect impacts us in every way possible.

The success I experienced fueled my desire to teach others about healthy living. I figured, if I can do it then I could show others how to follow suit. During my journey, God planted a passion in my heart to share my story, continue learning about health and nutrition, and to become a certified health coach.

My careless, selfish food habits, which held little regard for others or myself, are now a thing of the past. I look for ways to impact others and help them live a positive, enriched life. Each day I pray and ask, "Am I in step with what You want me to do today, Lord?"

• • •

To learn more about Cathy and find out about making healthy life choices, or for healthy recipes and tips, visit www.CathyChats.com. Also, check out her book, *A Life Course of Miracles and Prayer: Supernatural Events in Ordinary Lives.*

"The most difficult thing is the decision to act,
the rest is merely tenacity."
Amelia Earhart

For Prayerful Application

1. Have you, or will you, make a choice to honor God by taking care of your body through healthy eating habits?

> *"So whether you eat or drink or whatever you do;*
> *do it all for the glory of God."*
> 1 Corinthians 10:31 (NIV)

2. Do you believe God will give you strength, so you can make a choice to honor God with your body?

> *"Have I not commanded you? Be strong and courageous!*
> *Do not tremble or be dismayed, for the Lord your God*
> *is with you wherever you go."*
> Joshua 1:9 (NASB)

3. Read this scripture aloud, as a guideline in the journey choosing to live a healthy lifestyle:

> *"Rejoice in hope, be patient in tribulation,*
> *be constant in prayer."*
> Romans 12:12 (ESV)

PURPOSEFUL LIVING, DREAMS & GOALS

Living a Life of Purpose, Realizing God-Placed Dreams & Taking Action Steps

Purposeful Living, Dreams & Goals

Living a Life of Purpose,
Realizing God-Placed Dreams
& Taking Action Steps

THERE IS
ALWAYS
HOPE

One of the greatest gifts we have in life is to live a life of purpose. Indeed, God created us for a purpose. Our dreams are the seeds of purpose, and setting goals becomes the action plan to bring dreams to life. If you unpack the birth of a dream and the journey that follows, you cannot miss the fact God planted the dream. Dreams bring us great joy, and achieving goals brings fulfillment.

At times, the journey is scary. It's not easy to stretch outside of your comfort zone as you rise to the challenge of being the best you can be. Though hard, the journey is rewarding, fulfilling, and empowering. God, the One who fearfully designed you, has great plans for you.

> *"For I know the plans I have for you,*
> *declares the Lord,*
> *Plans to prosper you and not to harm you,*
> *Plans to give you hope and a future."*
> Jeremiah 29:11 (NIV)

Philippians 2:13 (ESV) tells us, "It is God who works in you, both to will and to work for His good pleasure." In Proverbs 19:21 (NIV), He says, "Many are the plans in a person's heart, but it is the Lord's purpose that prevails." When our personal goals clash with God's plan, we can find ourselves in a rebellious state, clamoring for what we feel is best. Or we can trust He knows and wants the best for us, and we can listen to Him and act on His guidance.

"For we are His workmanship,
created in Christ Jesus for good works,
which God prepared beforehand,
that we should walk in them."
Ephesians 2:10 (ESV)

God designed and called you to do good things in this world in the way only you uniquely can. Your life experiences, your skills, your gifts, and each of your stories have made you one of a kind. In Psalm 32:8, the Lord says He will instruct, teach, and counsel you in the way you should go.

In Isaiah 30:21, He says you will hear His voice behind you showing you the way. Can you trust Him to help you discover your purpose? Can you follow Him to walk fully in your purpose? God's purpose for your life is the most fulfilling and incredible experience you could have ever dreamed of!

"Trust in the Lord, and do good;
dwell in the land and cultivate faithfulness.
Delight yourself in the Lord,
and He will give you the desires of your heart."
Psalm 37:3, 4 (NASB)

As you allow God to untangle the threads of your life, it becomes clear that each experience is purposefully used for good. A mess becomes a message.

A weakness turns into a strength. I believe God starts planting desires within you at an early age and the steps toward your calling start unfolding and expanding as you grow into your purpose. Once you fully understand your journey, it is easy to see how Satan tries to counteract you, attempting to derail God's masterful plan for you. But God is stronger, and anything in Him cannot fail.

> *"And we know that for those who love God*
> *all things work together for good, for those who*
> *are called according to His purpose."*
> Romans 8:28 (ESV)

God's ultimate purpose is for every single one of us to have eternal life with Him. He wants us to live life fully, with joy on earth, and then in the afterlife with Him. He wants to be intimate with us and have a relationship with us. He wants us to know Him, and to experience His love.

> *"I in them and You in Me,*
> *that they may become perfectly one,*
> *so that the world may know that You sent me*
> *and loved them even as You loved me."*
> John 17:23 (ESV)

When you know God's love, you are compelled to share it. You step into your unique purpose of working with Him to make a difference in the world, doing all you can to further His love to others.

"Love the Lord your God with all your heart and with all your soul and with all your mind and with all your strength. The second is this: Love your neighbor as yourself. There is no commandment greater than these."
Mark 12:30-32 (NIV)

Some people know their purpose and intrinsically drive toward it from a young age. For most, finding purpose is a journey that takes time to develop, unfold, and expand from one experience to the next. Each event becomes a stepping-stone, and slowly, clarity and refining come. As you find God's will and His incredible purpose for your life, listen and wait to hear the action steps.

Prayerfully come before the Lord and ask Him to open your heart and mind to see the dreams He planted deep within you, the ones you have tucked away. Become aware of the desires of your heart.

Create a vision board. Be bold. Find pictures or draw them. Flow wherever your creativity allows you to go, and format it onto your vision board. Map out what lies ahead. What falls on the thirty, sixty, and ninety-day timeline? What waits for you in the future, in a yet unknown date? Create action steps for immediate dreams, and set up SMART goals. Keep your visual before you daily.

Neuroscience proves that you will realize what you focus on. Your brain makes connections wherever you focus, and new neuronal networks and pathways form during what is called neuroplasticity. Quantum physics teaches that we generate energetic frequencies or vibrations. We project energy in our emotions and thoughts when we focus on a particular goal. Our minds figure out how to reach goals. New chemical links establish a brain network when we consistently and repetitively focus on our aims.

Dr. Dave Krueger speaks about dissonance in his book, *Outsmart Your Brain*. Dissonance is tension in your brain caused from striving to move from where you are now to where you want to be, as you see your vision before you. Your brain hates a vacuum and will do all it can to close the gap. Dissonance creates motivation and results in a subconscious striving until achievement of vision and dreams.

During the process of dissonance, the brain faces resistance stemming from limiting beliefs, fear, low self-worth, and negative aspects of personality, which take root in childhood experiences. It is essential to allow God to heal you through daily devotions in His Word and meditation in prayer and as you move forward.

Listen to what God is saying. What experiences and people is He bringing to mind? What does He reveal? Acknowledge any pain, anger, fear, and unforgiveness you hold. Confess, ask Him to forgive you, heal you, and remove any hindrances.

Thank God for answering your prayer. Accept He has removed all negativity from you. Each time He removes a thread from your past, there's new room for Him to pour a little more of Himself into you, to heal you, and amplify the wonder of His creation.

Dreaming, setting goals, facing dissonance, and receiving healing from God is what strengthens and empowers you for God's purpose.

God's purpose for your life is not merely about activity; it's about you and God. It is about you growing into fullness and His likeness, to give His life to a hopeless world.

"But I have raised you up for this very purpose,
that I might show you My power and
that My name might be proclaimed in all the earth."
Exodus 9:16 (NIV)

As you ask God to show you the dreams in your heart, and as you place those dreams before you every day, incorporate all your senses into realizing your vision. Fully experience your dreams and goals in your mind.

Imagine where you are, who is with you, what you're wearing, the sounds you hear, the time of day, and most importantly the *feeling* you have when your dream becomes your reality. See your vision with more than a picture in your mind. Experience every detail. Our brains are wired to move toward what we envision as our reality. Our brains do not differentiate between sensory thoughts and reality.

As you set SMART Goals (see the Appendix for more on SMART Goals) write the goals and steps down in a notebook. This one simple act of writing will spark your subconscious mind and begin the flow to reaching your dreams

"Then the LORD answered me and said:
'Write the vision and make it plain on tablets,
That he may run who reads it.'"
Habakkuk 2:2 (NKJV)

As you create your timeline, be unattached to the outcome. It is important to be mindful of what is still unseen to you, yet seen to God. Your timing and God's timing are not always in sync. He sees the big picture and all the in-between steps required to achieve the outcome.

The road is seldom straight. It meanders, as there are so many details to emerge. Often, you are the one who needs to grow to fully achieve your goals. At times, other people may also impact your journey.

Have faith! Believe you are called for a purpose, for your specific purpose, and that God is in it and will see you through. Proverbs 16:3 says, "Commit your work to the Lord, and your plans will be established." Hebrews 11:1 says faith is having confidence in what we hope for, having assurance in what we do not see.

"And I am sure of this,
that he who began a good work in you
will bring it to completion at the day of Jesus Christ."
Philippians 1:6 (ESV)

"When I stand before God at the end of my life,
I would hope that I would not have a
single bit of talent left and could say,
I used everything you gave me."
Erma Bombeck

Powerful God, Powerful Purpose

Purposeful Living, Dreams & Goals

Juanita Kretschmar

THERE IS
ALWAYS
HOPE

True to form, the first thing we did before sharing stories was to kneel and invite the Holy Spirit's presence to be with us. Even Juanita's dachshund has a prayer cushion and comes to pray!

I remember meeting and visiting Juanita in New York City many years back where she taught me about the Holy Spirit. In the years that followed, she taught me about the power of prayer and developing a personal relationship with Jesus. She has been one of my greatest mentors and prayer warriors. It has been my honor to work alongside her, pray with her, and pray for her. She is truly a woman who walks with God and one who gives without ceasing to Jesus and others.

Throughout her life, Juanita has never wavered from her commitment to her purpose to know God and share Him so others can find peace in their lives and discover His love. No matter her earthly losses, she remains firm in her love, obedience, and service to God, ever giving to Him and others.

• • •

I had a thirst to know God and was compelled to share Him so others could discover His love and find peace in their lives. For many years, I shared in my husband's ministry, serving as a pastor's wife and in various other ministries. The more I gave, the more God would pour out His abundant Spirit.

My waking custom each morning is to ask the Holy Spirit to enter my life. I open my Bible and ask Him to speak to me. Sometimes God prepares me and reveals His will, and other times He does not. I continued to give my life and time to God and service through the events of life. In return, God poured out comfort, guidance, and peace.

While we were still living in New York, our youngest son, George, was at the University of Michigan working on a Masters of Divinity degree. My husband had invited me to go with him to Thailand and Indonesia. A few days before we left, a call came through that George was in the hospital.

Our son had gone to a health fair where he had a blood test done. The clinicians promptly sent him off to the hospital with the discovery of a terminal disease. He was twenty-six years old with a prognosis of five years to live.

We went on our trip with heavy hearts. A lady from our group on the trip began to talk to me about her son's death. He had the same rare disease George had. At that moment, I realized the Lord was preparing me to lose my son.

For years, each time George became ill, we would rush to his side for a season of prayer, and he would bounce back. We continued to have faith, believing God would heal our son and give him a long life.

During one of my well-established, rhythmic morning times of fellowship with God, the Holy Spirit impressed in my spirit that George's next episode of illness would be his last.

Scripture after scripture indicated the same message: *"You will bury these young bones ..."* I wept my way through my devotion but felt not to share what I heard with anyone. It had been 12 years since his original diagnosis. He had already outlived the five-year prognosis; God could continue to spare his life.

I did not tell my husband what the Lord spoke to me that day. It would dash his faith, and he believed so strongly God would heal our son. Just like my husband, I also had strong faith in Jesus and knew that He could heal George. My husband and I had seen many healings in our time in ministry. We both desperately longed to see our son receive a miracle, but God told me differently. I knew what was to come.

It wasn't long after that when, on top of everything else, doctors diagnosed George with cancer. He was not eligible for a transplant. I held back my tears when I was around other people. My son couldn't understand why I didn't cry, but I didn't want to discourage him or take away his hope. He was only 38-years-old.

He asked me to pray with him, and God gave me the strength to pray in faith.

George's wife once asked me, "Mom, what's going to happen to me?" I tried to comfort her, and silently I began to cry until I had no more tears.

During the hours when his life was drawing to a close, I heard a song in my head that sounded like a chorus of angels. The song was: *"We have heard a joyful sound, Jesus saves! Jesus saves!"* I heard those joyous voices of victory resound in my head for hours!

We gathered around George's bed as he lay dying in ICU. I shared with everyone the song I was hearing. I knew Jesus was telling me, *"George is safe; you can be at peace."*

During the teenage years when George was still goofing off, I often prayed, *"Do whatever You must, but please, Jesus, save my son."* He had already given his life to Christ at the time of his diagnosis, and he continued to live the remainder of his life passionately serving young people and leading many to know Jesus.

A crowd of young people George had ministered to was gathered in the hospital waiting room. I went down to meet with them, and told them about the angels singing, *"Jesus saves!"* I asked those kids to be sure to be at the resurrection when we would all be reunited with George once again.

When George died, a great emptiness filled me. I felt lonely as we prepared for the burial. It was Christmas time, and it was hard to see others find joy when my son had just died.

After that, I worked for nine months to write and produce a program called *The Ultimate Encounter,* which we would share through a part of our ministry at a planetarium in the Florida Keys. A friend sent us recordings of the last sermons George had preached at his pastorate in Maryland before he died. We copied his sermons and gave them as gifts to guests that came through *The Ultimate Encounter* program. As I prepared the sermons for distribution, I broke down and sobbed my heart out.

My husband, Merlin, used to ask, *"How are you so strong?"*

I told him I was not strong, but that rather God had been preparing me. I told Merlin how I sobbed and prayed morning after morning in the weeks before George died. I told him how I asked God if there was another way.

I believe God gave me strength in my prayer time, and knowledge of what was to come, so I could be there for my husband, daughter, son, and the families. I said, *"All things work together for good!"* We still loved and missed George, but we knew he was safe in the arms of Jesus.

In 2007, my husband and I were having breakfast together when I experienced another loss. This time, God had not prepared me ahead of time, and it happened quickly. A massive heart attack took my Merlin from life one minute, to death the next.

We had been together 24/7 in retirement working as a pastoral team. I remember walking into our bedroom that first night and saying, "I don't know if I can do this, live alone and run a ministry by myself."

I heard the voice of the Lord say, *"But this is better for Merlin."*

It was the best thing God could have said to me. Merlin always said that when he died, he wanted to go quickly, and not be a burden to me. He said he knew I wouldn't stop working for God, even if I were his caretaker if he were ill. He didn't want to see me strained. He cared so deeply for me and God's work.

Everything in my life changed the day Merlin died, except for one thing—my early morning time with God.

In the days that followed, loss set in and grief enveloped me. One day, I went to the store and began looking to see which aisle Merlin was in. It was as if I forgot he wasn't there. Suddenly it hit me; he was gone forever as far as life on earth was concerned.

I looked up at the ceiling and said, *"If he can't be with me, I don't want to go on either!"* I was married for fifty-four years, and now I was learning what it was to be single. It wasn't easy.

Immediately, the same words I use when I counsel others came to my mind and flowed from my lips. *"I reject what I just said by the power of the blood of Jesus Christ."*

I was determined not to reject the life God had given me. Enabled by Christ's strength, I would make it through each day.

On another occasion, at a church luncheon after getting my food, I looked around as I always had to see where Merlin was. Suddenly, I realized he wasn't there and would never again be there. As if reliving the initial shock, I slammed my hand down on the counter. I told myself, *"He'll never be here again."*

The churches Merlin and I pastored together asked me to continue pastoring. I didn't want to. Merlin was always the lead pastor. Eventually, God made it clear He was displeased with my "no" answer and gave me the strength to step up and lead. In the months that followed, my obedience to God facilitated my being able to hear Him clearly when He spoke. *"Get on the radio!"* He said, which eventually led to me accepting a slot on a radio station.

Throughout my life, my walk with God has deepened, and I've learned so much more about Him.

There have been many times I didn't want to hear the scriptures of Christ's second coming *someday*; I wanted Him to come *now*.

I claimed words of wisdom and the whispers God spoke to my heart.

"Don't' be afraid. I'm with you."

"God's middle name is Mercy. He is so merciful to us."

Sometimes God prepares us and reveals His will, and other times He does not. One thing I know, He will not give us more than we can handle with Him!

My love story with Jesus has never ended. Ours is an hourly, daily relationship that always has me asking, "What do You want? What is the message You want to share through me?"

. . .

For more about Juanita's ministry, request her free newsletter by writing to P.O. Box 177, Big Pine Key, FL 33043.

Listen to her radio ministry "Whole Health 'N Joyful News: Christ is coming!" on 95.7 FM, or online at whnj.org.

Contact Juanita for a free copy of her magazine, *Power to Cope*, while supplies last.

For Prayerful Application

1. Do the perplexities of life, your deepest heartache or mere busyness of each day prevent you from spending daily, intimate time with Jesus? Does your busy life derail you from giving to fulfill your purpose?

"I can do all things through Christ who strengthens me."
Philippians 4:13 (NKJV)

"Throw off everything that hinders . . . and run with perseverance the race marked out for us."
Hebrews 12:1 (NIV)

2. Have you ever had a time in your life when you felt overwhelmed or at the end of your rope, not knowing how to face another day? Know that He is with you and will see you through.

"I bore you on eagles' wings, and brought you to Myself."
Exodus 19:4 (NASB)

3. Do you trust Jesus to meet your every need, more than you could ever have imagined, as you give to Him relentlessly?

"Give, and it will be given to you."
Luke 6:38 (NIV)

"Our prayers are not to be a selfish asking, merely for our own benefit. We are to ask that we may give. The principle of Christ's life must be the principle of our lives. For their sakes."
Ellen G. White

Expanding the Dream & Territory

Purposeful Living, Dreams & Goals

Sarah Huxford

THERE IS
ALWAYS
HOPE

I was filled with wonder as music filled every corner of my being. The lighting and crowd took my breath away. The preacher was down to earth with his slight Southern drawl, as well as practical and humorous. The people friendly, warm, and embracing.

I wondered if I'd get lost in this big church, but thankfully I was drawn into a small group and the monthly women's ministry, REAL Time.

Sarah, the tall, long-haired, blonde commanded the lead, and it immediately became apparent she knew the Scriptures and was incredibly creative. I've seen the work, dedication, and commitment of this pastor's wife and minister, Sarah Huxford, to Jesus, her family, and church.

• • •

I made a decision to live for the Lord when I was very young. Loving Him was easy. I was the fifth child in an amazing family who took God seriously and stayed steeped in His Word.

My big dream was to become a dolphin trainer. During my high school years in California, I so loved the ocean. I was a swimmer and a lifeguard, checking out colleges like Scripps Institute of Oceanography and a dolphinarium in Sweden.

One day, it dawned on me I couldn't save a dolphin's soul, and I was created to be a part of Jesus' work to save souls. I decided to pursue ministry and intended to stay single and serve the Lord. It was not common for women to pursue ministry, and, if one did, people often considered it mostly as husband-seeking.

My story was different. I had an aunt who was a missionary and lived solely for the Lord. She inspired me immensely and showed me it was possible for a woman to be powerfully used in ministry.

In response to answering God's call on my life, my search for a college changed. The first education opportunity I said "yes" to was a ministry called Torchbearers. I loved their premise of giving students a year to study the Bible no matter what field they were going into. I loved that focused year!

I continued to work with the Torchbearers ministry for several years as the Waterfront Director training lifeguards. It was a great need, as there were many pool and river activities for campers of all ages.

I continued to prepare for whatever mission field God had for me at a small but remarkable Christian Liberal Arts College, Milligan College. I earned an education degree and a ministry degree there.

I knew I would never marry unless I found someone who loved my Lord Jesus as much as I did. While at Milligan College, I met a young man named Cam Huxford, who attended the seminary across the street.

Cam, strangely enough, had the same prerequisite for marriage as I did. He had a great love for the Lord.

What fun it was getting to know a man who loved the Lord more than I did. We started to get the sneaking feeling God might be able to do more with us together than separately. Plus, we were crazy about each other!

Cam was in graduate school, worked as a college recruiter, and traveled as a youth speaker. It wasn't long before a church in Rock Hill, South Carolina voted him in as the pastor. It was a brave move as the church recently split and was in need of healing and recovery. We married and poured our hearts and souls into ministry. God blessed by allowing us to see the church double in size in one year.

We were invited to speak at a youth revival at Savannah Christian Church in Georgia. The church had 250 members, and we thought it was huge! We loved the church from that first experience.

The church called Cam three times asking him to serve as their youth pastor, but we knew Cam was called to preach and wouldn't be focusing his entire ministry on youth. He was already serving as the lead pastor at our church in South Carolina, and we felt we couldn't say yes to a youth pastor position, no matter how much we wanted the change.

Between the two of us, we agreed to serve our small church wholeheartedly for six months, and wait to see what God had in store. On the exact day the six months ended, Savannah Christian Church called again—this time asking Cam to be the lead pastor. They gave strict instructions we were not to tell the congregation his age until he turned thirty. We were "too young for a church this size." We knew it was God's will for us to pastor the church in Savannah and agreed not to tell anyone they had called a pastor still in his twenties!

We have now been serving the Savannah community for 33 years. Once God gave the vision and the call, we had the power to answer. Many days were tough, and some people weren't happy with the situation. But, when you're following God, people can't buy you off, and they can't run you off because you're answering to God.

In our younger years, it was easy to say to God, "We'll go anywhere. We'll do anything. We want to be Your people." Interestingly, throughout our years of ministry, God has asked these questions: "Are you still ready to go anywhere? Are you still willing to do anything? Are you still mine?" We never know in what season He will bring up a new call or new direction, but I love how He continually makes things new. He reminds us it's not about "our" church or "our" work. It's about Him.

We thought God would eventually call us to be church planters out West. As we asked God, "What's next?" He continually, quietly answered, "Will you stay here?"

The first decade was hard. The second decade was a little easier. Now, in our third decade, we're so blessed. I always wanted a church full of people who say, "This is our church! This is our Family!" Truly our church IS everyone's church and great family.

The Lord gave my husband a big vision early on, and I followed along wholeheartedly, but I didn't see the vision as clearly as he did all those years ago. People always ask, "Did you ever dream your church would be this size?" Cam always answers, "Yes." He had seen it and dreamed about it years ago.

God blessed Cam and me with three sons, each two years apart. We knew they would face hardship growing up with the complexities all preacher's kids endure, such as the demands of ministry on the family. We prayed daily that our boys would not resent the ministry. I watched as the good people of our church helped mentor the kids, pour into them, and surround them. The church helped raise our children. I am so thankful for all the other good voices that spoke into their lives through the years. Kids all need someone outside of their parents.

We wanted our boys to love their church, but we never encouraged them toward pursuing church work or ministry. We prayed our kids would find Jesus, hear His call, and follow His choice for each of their lives. Surprisingly, all three grew up to pursue ministry! I see that as a huge blessing and gift from God. I love watching them serve God wholeheartedly. How precious it has been watching God's call on their lives. I remember hearing one of them say, "If God doesn't have all of me, He doesn't have any of me." For a parent, it doesn't get much better than that.

I faced a great challenge when the boys were in grade school, and I was still in my thirties. Doctors diagnosed me with cancer, which was rare at my young age in those years. I remember the day they stamped "the big C" on me. Our lives changed radically.

It was the first time I didn't know how to pray for myself. My prayers felt inadequate. I tried to spend time with the Lord, but I had no words. In my determination to fellowship with God, I would sing praise choruses during my quiet time each morning. I would also sing during treatments.

My only prayer was, "Father, I would like to see my boys get big." My youngest was just a little boy. I'd look at him and pray that same prayer over and over. Now, he is six-foot-five! When that big man walks in, I see an answered prayer; I did see him get big.

Before my illness, we didn't really know how much our congregation loved us. When cancer engulfed our lives, we could see, hear, and feel their love and care. They showed up for us. They overwhelmed us with their love. When you're loved and cared for well, you realize how it touches your life. My cancer diagnosis changed us. It cemented us together with our church.

I would not change the fact that I had cancer, nor would I choose to have it again; however, after I experienced how the Lord could bring me out of such hopelessness, my thinking changed. I wouldn't trade my personal experience, nor change what God did in our church through it all.

I believe even my boys grew through the experience. I didn't want my boys to come home from school to a sick mom, but they did—even though I tried to act like I wasn't sick. God used the very thing I didn't want to happen. Having a mom with cancer gave my boys an enormous capacity for compassion.

I am now 20 years cancer free, and I don't know what lies ahead, except to trust God no matter what. I believe the cancer part of our story, was a part of the foundation for what God was building these past twenty years. It has been an honor to be a part of a mega church which now has seven campuses, 76 global partners, and 128,025 viewers online last year. How can I not say "Thank You" to the Lord for keeping us here?

Through the years, I have done whatever needed for that season in our church. I've worked everywhere from the kitchen team to college ministry, from music and drama production to middle school. My passion is to tell the story of Jesus in creative and unique ways. I wrote Christmas and Easter productions and youth musicals hoping to tell His story in new ways. My joy is to teach God's Word creatively through stories. I love to create something new that might break down barriers so others can hear about Jesus and His life-saving grace.

After a while, I transitioned out of the production and drama ministries so I could partner with Cam more strategically. Cam and I have always believed that helping grow strong and healthy families is the job of the church. Our God is a family builder, and He uses His people to sharpen each other.

With our focus on families, I took on the role of Women's Pastor and launched REAL Women Ministries. A significant part of my work is answering many questions about marriage. My passion for helping build strong marriages, combined with my love of creative story-telling, led me to write *The Harley Chronicles: Everything I Learned about my Marriage on the Back of a Harley*. And, yes, my back-seat on Cam's Harley opened the door for many marriage lessons! I paired stories from our marriage with principals from Genesis to

Revelation to allow the Bible to speak into lives about marriage.

I'm so thankful my heart's focus is on my sweet Jesus. I choose nothing else, but to live in His purpose and call for my life—to share the Gospel every day, in every way, with everyone.

Thank You, Jesus, for who You are and for what You do for each of us!

• • •

To learn more about Sarah and Cam's Ministry, visit www.CompassionChristian.com.

To purchase her book, *The Harley Chronicles: Everything I Learned about my Marriage on the Back of a Harley*, visit www.SarahHuxford.com.

Follow Sarah's blog for encouragement, inspiration, and teaching.

For Prayerful Application

1. Building a strong marriage requires work. Do you believe God created marriage to strengthen each person, teach respect, and show His love through the relationship?

> *"Be completely humble and gentle; be patient, bearing with one another in love. Make every effort to keep the unity of the Spirit through the bond of peace."*
> Ephesians 4:2-3 (NIV)

> *"Be kind to one another, tenderhearted, forgiving one another, as God in Christ forgave you."*
> Ephesians 4:23 (ESV)

2. Do you believe we are stronger together, be it in marriage or with ministry partners?

> *"Two are better than one, because they have a good return for their labor. If either of them falls down, one can help the other up. But pity anyone who falls and has no one to help him up! Also, if two lie down together, they will keep warm. But how can one keep warm alone? Though one may be overpowered, two can defend themselves. A cord of three strands is not quickly broken."*
> Ecclesiastes 4:9-12 (NIV)

3. Will you allow God to be with you in each trial or obstacle you face? Do you know He will see you through and will use everything for His ultimate good both in your life and others' lives?

"No temptation has overtaken you except such as is common to mankind. And God is faithful; He will not let you be tempted beyond what you can bear. But when you are tempted, He will also provide a way that you can endure it."
1 Corinthians 10:13 (NIV)

"We will never be happy until we make God the source of our fulfillment and the answer to our longings. He is the only one who should have power over our souls."
Stormie Omartian

Redemption, Restoration & Relationship

Purposeful Living, Dreams & Goals

THERE IS
ALWAYS
HOPE

Pam Wolf

Petite with blonde hair, big eyes and porcelain skin, her elegance is completed with her warm, embracing smile. My heart rejoices at the sight of her every time we meet. We met as colleagues in the coaching world, but she soon became a mentor, my coach, and friend. I felt privileged to hear her story as we sat in her beautiful home. The Holy Spirit moved, and praise and awe filled our hearts as we felt His incredible, extravagant generosity.

• • •

Mine is a story of the restoration and redemption of relationships. What was lost is now found, and what was damaged is now repaired. Jesus keeps redeeming and restoring over and over again, and His work is exceedingly abundant.

I do not forget or devalue the past, but I turn to Jesus as He says, "Look and see what I can do." I wonder if I could truly appreciate Him without experiencing struggle. I do not think victory would be as sweet. Through trials, appreciation wells from a deep and very real place within me.

My entrepreneurial parents gave me three gifts. They taught me how to work hard, to believe in myself, and know good things are possible. Sadly, they divorced when I was five—a rare occurrence in the early 1950's. I processed the divorce by striving to work hard, and becoming a perfectionist. I was athletic, a cheerleader, always the captain and leader. It seemed I was wired to be at the top.

At age twelve, I decided to become a lawyer. I thought it was an exciting profession where I could make money. I knew I could reach my dream, even though the era of the "glass ceiling" told me wives and mothers couldn't be lawyers too. "You can be a teacher or a nurse," they said. Over time, I believed them, and instead of law school, I started nursing school. My pursuit lasted for only a year and I realized nursing was not for me.

I changed majors to teaching, which lasted five days. Frustrated and confused, I went to the academic guidance counselor and asked what I should do. "A good basic business degree will serve you well. Instead of being a nurse or a teacher, perhaps you could run the hospital?" As I began my course of study in finance and management, I felt like a duck that found the right pond. I knew I was meant for business.

My dad's entrepreneurial spirit led him to build a large Pest Control business. Once I graduated, he asked me to come and work in the family business for a year. In return, he would pay for me to go back to school and pursue a law degree, which I still yearned after.

I humbly started as the payroll clerk earning minimum wage. I worked from the ground floor up and learned the business. Six months in, my dad had a heart attack and passed away.

At age twenty-four, I was the heir to the business. I thought I would sell it, and move on with my life. I knew my dad was a phenomenal salesman, an entrepreneur ahead of his time, but after he had died, I learned he was not quite as good when it came to managing business finances. I discovered the company owed more than it was worth, was technically bankrupt, and could not be sold.

My only option was to do a business turn-around. It took about three years to pay off the debt, and by that time I had fallen in love with the fast-paced, people-oriented business. In 1979, we brought in about three million dollars. I stayed and built the business twelve more years. At that time, there were only two women in the US who owned pest-control businesses, and I was one of them. When I sold the business to Waste Management for $20 million, we were one of the ten largest closely held companies in the nation, with thirteen offices and over three hundred employees.

I quickly learned my strident, independent, "watch-me-roll" spirit served me well in the business world. I was the Iron Woman, the "hear me roar lady." It took me a long time to realize that independence proved to be more complex, and unsuccessful, in personal relationships.

I married in my late twenties and had two beautiful children, Nicholas and Amanda. Their father was always the life of the party, easy going, and everything I wasn't. Eventually, our differences led to both marital and financial strain. Rather than find ways to work through it, we moved on and divorced when the children were six and three years old.

Divorce was the one thing I never wanted, yet all the advice from my family, friends, and advisors said, "You've got a good job. You've got a good income. You can do life by yourself." When I look back, there were a lot of "worldly" reasons to leave the marriage, yet not one person challenged us to find a way to make it work. It never occurred to me to honor or value the covenant I made. I'm not blaming others for their advice, or lack of it; that was just the way of the world. "If it feels good, do it." Anything that doesn't make you "happy" is disposable.

At that time, I had no idea I could approach life differently, or in a better way. I had yet to find the power and guidance of the Holy Spirit, the wisdom of Scripture, or the knowledge of the truth that God hates divorce for a good reason. Even though God can always weave the broken pieces of our lives together for good, there are consequences to every choice we make. Where there's sin, there's death.

When we do not honor God's covenant, we come out from under His order of authority, and we move away from His greatest level of protection and blessing. When I chose the path of divorce, the result was the death of a family and death of a marriage. I was still under the notion that if the parents could get along well after the divorce, the children would be unaffected. Looking back now, I know that is NOT TRUE.

My children tell me the thing they hated most was constantly having to choose between parents. I didn't realize the strain and impact divorce has on children. The kids don't get to vote when it comes to divorce; they have no voice. Divorce is sad, changes them, and they experience the collateral damage. How deeply thankful I am for God's miraculous mercy in working a great deal of supernatural healing and redemption in our lives.

After the divorce, I went on to build another successful business in brokering. Back at my "safe place," work was my hideout. My career gave me the validation I sought as my personal life continued on rocky ground.

Then I met Tom. It was love at first sight. He was a serial entrepreneur; we were cut from the same cloth. He had a great corporate resume, but, like me, he also had a trail of destruction in his personal life. Somehow I was able to overlook his "mess," just as I overlooked mine. One of the greatest aspects of our lives that drew us together was our role as parents, and our desire to piece a family back together. He had a daughter he adored, and I had my two children. As the years passed, our three kids have learned to genuinely love each other as if they were brother and sisters.

Our marriage was filled with determination as we struggled through the rough, early years of blending families. We agreed failure wasn't an option and we would work through the tough times no matter what. We wanted to show our kids marriage can work. But, oh, my! In the beginning, it was a frightening thing as we didn't yet know Jesus. We did everything in our strength, and it was EXHAUSTING!

In all honesty, at this point, my life story looked more like a train wreck than a fairy tale. Humpty Dumpty had fallen. I was a broken woman and wanted Tom to come and fix what life had destroyed.

Eventually, I realized my desire was not possible. Still, I pursued a fairy tale. I had sworn to myself Tom was to be Prince Charming. As we each continued to build growing careers, together we built our dream home while trying to restore peace to our family.

Around that time, the God I did not yet know began to woo me and show me blessings were flowing beyond what I could accomplish alone. I looked heavenward and knew there must be a God up there somewhere. Without fully realizing or understanding it, God had deeply touched and stirred my soul.

Amidst our increasingly beautiful, but fragile, new life, trouble brewed. In his junior year, my son, who was my joy, entered the world of drugs and alcohol. His problem became serious. No matter what we did, from discipline to grounding, to his dad intervening, Tom and I could not reach Nicolas. My soul was in despair, and darkness overwhelmed me.

I continued to work while hiding the huge hole in my heart. Then, at a Christmas party, a lady invited me to a Bible study group in our new neighborhood. I had never heard of having a personal relationship with God. I considered the Bible just one more book to (maybe) read. I contemplated attending the Bible study and wondered if I would fit in. Would they think less of me, with my history of divorce and my struggling son? Would I be the woman with the big red "S" for "sin" on my forehead?

Again, the Holy Spirit was wooing me. I was 47-years-old, and He had never given up on me. He kept pursuing me, drawing me. Interestingly, the Bible study was about the fruit of the Spirit. The lady leading the study was named Grace (God really does have a sense of humor). I remember going up to her afterward saying, "If this is what it takes to be a Christian, I can never be or do all these things."

She looked lovingly into my eyes and said, "Pam, you don't have to do it alone. You can have the power of the Holy Spirit to help you."

I didn't understand what she meant. Intellectually, I wanted to have the power of the Holy Spirit. I was determined to wrap my mind around the concepts, and believed I could develop the fruit of the Spirit. This time, God used my determination in such a different way than ever before.

I continued to attend the Bible study and began to listen to a Christian program on the radio. One morning as I drove, I heard the radio teacher say, "A little bit of yeast in dough affects the whole lump and causes it to rise. The same happens with sin. A little bit of sin can spread and affect other areas of life."

Instantly, God brought to my mind the memory of the dream I had the night before. I was baking bread with my grandma, just as I did as a little girl. The bread kept rising and rising, and I was handing it to my youngest daughter to help me. Over and over again, we tried to keep up with the rising dough. Listening to that Bible study, I realized I was handing my daughter the ways of the world. I broke down and cried so hard I had to pull off the side of the road. The Lord was allowing my heart to understand the things that break His!

My son had already left for college and was continuing to indulge in harmful behavior I couldn't fix, but my daughter was still home attending high school. God was saying to me, "You still have time!" Later that day as I read the book of Joel, God assured me He would restore the years of my life that were destroyed. He would not use a fictional Prince Charming, but God Himself would supernaturally restore my life. God was speaking to me, and for the first time, I was pretty sure I could hear Him!

I could not wait to go to the next Bible study. Boldly, I burst out, "Grace! Grace! I think God's talking to me even in dreams! Is that Him?"

"Oh, yeah! That would be Him!" She said.

It was on that day, June 13, 2001, I invited Jesus into my heart to be my Lord and Savior. Then, as only God could do, 30 days later my husband became a Christian. Amazement and gratitude flood my soul still to this day, and nothing has been the same since.

In the two years that followed, I stayed under Grace's wing of discipleship. I spent eight years in the Bible Study Fellowship. Over the years, I learned I could find everything I needed in the Bible. That Book shows the better way to do life and gives me everything I need to teach my children. What a gift!

Did everything turn around at once? No. Life, even for a believer, is a journey.

Following our conversion, my son spent ten years in a dark, spiraling addiction. In the midst of the pain, God assured me He heard my prayer and my son's salvation was sure to come. Through it all, I learned to know God, to trust Him, and believe what He says is true. During the ravages of a loved one's addiction, the only thing you can do is trust God to bring you through.

Over time, God gave me the courage to attend a Celebrate Recovery twelve-step program, where I began to recognize my struggle with co-dependency, rescuing, and enabling. I had to stop bailing my son out of his troubles and paying his bills. Even though I gave help from a deep place of love, God made it clear if I didn't allow my son to suffer the consequences of his decisions, he would never break free from them. I was making it easier for Nicolas to stay in his lifestyle.

Finally, I said, "Lord, I trust You enough to put my son in Your hands." I reached my own "laying Isaac down" moment. My son was and is a gift from God, and I had to steward him wisely.

Five years into his addiction, on his 21st birthday, I remember I didn't know if he was dead or alive. I pled with God, "Father, I don't know where my son is, but I give Him to you. Do whatever it takes to bring him back to You."

God whispered back, "That's the prayer of a godly mother's heart that I've been waiting to hear."

My plea was no longer about me and making my life easier by God saving my son. I knew my son needed Jesus, the only hope. Little did I know, there were still five years ahead. Circumstances would go from bad to worse, yet God would assure me, "I know how much you love him. I love him more. I have him in the palm of my Hand."

There were a lot of dark moments to endure and at times I thought Nicolas might not be whole until Heaven, but I ultimately knew God would save Him. It has now been more than eight years since my son has been clean and sober without one relapse! He knows the only reason he stays sober is because of God, and that his journey is one day at a time. I am proud to say he put himself through school, married a beautiful woman, and became a father. The miracle of his healing and restoration still quiets my heart.

Through it all, our family survived and drew close to Jesus. Tom and Amanda were such a gift. They were my strength when I needed it. Amanda and I have been extraordinarily close, and not only love each other but have become best friends. Now she is an adult and young mama, and we have the joy of sharing the love of Jesus through all the struggles we go through as mothers and wives. I am so grateful that even through the destruction of addiction, our family had a beautiful outcome. It is interesting how God redeemed our sweet blended family and brought us into deep friendship and relationship.

Along the way, I longed for my step-daughter, Megan, to have an even greater space and place in our family. God brought our relationship into full bloom in two stages. First, during her teen years, and then later when she had her first baby. As we shared these special times together, we came to a new understanding of what love is, and God opened the door for a very special mom and step-daughter relationship to develop. God further honored my longing when Megan and her husband became born-again Christians. Being able to walk alongside them as young Christians has been such a close and special experience, a treasure. I am grateful all of our children now know Jesus.

Our journey of restoration continued as we went through a period of deep need and prayer for physical healing for my sweet daughter, Amanda. She was diagnosed with an aggressive cancer that left me begging and crying out to God, "Why her? Why this?"

Once again, God showed Himself real in my life and confirmed how much I could trust Him, even in the face of cancer. I believed God would heal Amanda. I knew if it wasn't for God's grace and sustaining power, I could not walk the journey in strength with her. God did see fit to perform a miracle in Amanda's life, and after grueling surgeries, chemo and radiation, she has recovered and is cancer free! She is a true miracle!

I have repeatedly experienced God's redemptive power in my life. It is with extreme gratitude that Tom and I have committed our lives to live out God's purpose for us, using the gifts and skills we've acquired over a lifetime. We know our lives, our stories, even our messes, hold meaning.

God has called Tom and me to coach, mentor, and teach others to find God's purpose for their lives. We are passionate about ministry and work harder and with more drive than ever. We have furthered our work by training facilitators to teach our program, which now reaches thousands globally. How could we not continue in this work for the Lord? It's all from Him, and for Him!

• • •

Tom and Pam Wolf are the founders of Tom & Pam Wolf Coaching and authors of the powerful book, *Finding Your Sweet Spot. Identity and Destiny — 7 Steps to a Purpose-Filled Life.* They are speakers, authors, and business success coaches who believe the discovery of your God-given purpose is the foundation on which all fruitful lives are built. For more about them, visit IdentityAndDestiny.com, or TomAndPamwolf.com.

"If human beings are perceived as potentials rather than problems, as possessing strengths instead of weaknesses, as unlimited rather than dull and unresponsive, then they thrive and grow their capabilities."
Barbara Bush

For Prayerful Application

1. Do you know and believe in your heart that Jesus can and will see you through whatever you are going through?

"We rejoice in our sufferings, knowing that suffering produces endurance, and endurance produces character, and character produces hope, and hope does not put us to shame."
Romans 5:3-5 (ESV)

2. Are you co-dependent, needing control and having to fix what's not working in a situation, a relationship, or a person you love? Can you let go and trust God with what you are trying to control?

"Give all your worries to God, for He cares about you."
1 Peter 5:7 (NLT)

"Come to Me, all who labor and are heavy laden, and I will give you rest."
Matthew 11:28 (ESV)

3. Do you know God has a purpose for your life? Do you see how God wants to use your gifts, talents, story, and maybe even your mess?

"For I know the thoughts and plans I have for you, says the Lord, thoughts and plans for welfare and peace and not for evil, to give you hope in your final outcome."
Jeremiah 29:11 (AMP)

ESSENTIAL LIFE SKILL 5

THE ART OF GIVING

Practicing Giving & Forgiveness
To God, Others & Yourself

The Art of Giving
Practicing Giving & Forgiveness
To God, Others & Yourself

THERE IS
ALWAYS
HOPE

God created, designed, and wired you to give. God made you in His image, and He is the Ultimate Giver. Does your giving hurt and hinder, or help and give hope? What do you give? Who do you give it to? When, where, why, and how do you give?

There is a simple yet profound art to the act of giving. True giving—artful giving—flows from a heart of thankfulness. You can't help but give because your heart overflows with thanks.

The amount you give may come and go like waves responding to events in your life. At times, you may give out of joy and abundance. In other seasons, you may give from your sadness and experience healing as a result of giving. The greatest healing gift you can give yourself is to forgive.

Without forgiveness, anger harbors deep within your soul and continues to grow. Anger leads to bitterness and develops into fear, creating limiting beliefs. Satan uses the negative space in your soul, heart, and mind to manipulate your thinking. Ultimately, a lack of forgiveness will destroy you, blocking you behind a wall that separates you from God, future growth, peace, and heartfelt joy.

Mark 11:25 (NIV) tells us, "And when you stand praying, if you hold anything against anyone, forgive them, so that your Father in heaven may forgive you your sins."

"Get rid of all bitterness, rage, and anger,
brawling and slander, along with every form of malice.
Be kind and compassionate to one another,
forgiving each other, just as in Christ, God forgave you."
Ephesians 4:31, 32 (NIV)

An intimate relationship with God results in abundant giving, which consistently flows regardless of circumstance. As you experience God's grace in your life, you are compelled to give grace, encouragement, and life-giving HOPE to others. Your giving may be in the form of words, actions, gifts, or prayers. Give in the way God created you to give, and you will fulfill your purpose. You will show the world His story through your life.

Each of the four previous life skills leads to giving. When you control your thoughts and your tongue by not complaining, you give by creating a positive atmosphere for growth. When you love who you are and accept who God created you to be, your affirmations turn into thanks and praise, enabling you to give encouragement to yourself and others.

When you choose to live a healthy lifestyle, your attitude, energy, and courage soar, allowing you to give with vitality and joy. Living in your purpose, achieving your dreams, and accomplishing your goals, always results in giving to make a difference in the lives of others.

"A generous person will prosper;
Whoever refreshes others will be refreshed."
Proverbs 11:25 (AMP)

The act of giving is in and of itself a gift. You cannot give without receiving in return. In Luke 6:38, Jesus said, "Give, and it will be given to you." It's not that we give to receive, but that it just happens because it's God's way. Often we think of receiving in terms of the tangible—money, cars, houses, or bills paid. Yet, often our giving results in receiving the invisible, but greater, gifts of peace, joy, contentment, dreams, hope, and opportunity.

The greatest gift that flows from giving is eternal life. When we give of ourselves to further the gospel, we give for eternity and store up treasure in Heaven. Each act of giving has an eternal purpose. In return, we receive strength, courage, motivation, sustaining power, and purity!

"Do not store up for yourselves treasures on earth, where
moth and rust destroy, and where thieves break in and steal.
But store up for yourselves treasures in heaven, where moth
and rust do not destroy, and where thieves do not break in
and steal. Where your treasure is your heart will be also."
Matthew 6:19-21 (NASB)

"Behold, I am coming quickly, and My reward is with Me, to
render to every man according to what he has done."
Revelation 22:12 (NASB)

What have you done? What do you do? What do you give? Consider giving in a variety of ways:

1. *Time for God:* First things first! The time you spend in relationship with God is first priority. The time you give God indicates a life changed through His power. Give God the first and last bit of time each day. Spend time in God's Word, and in prayer and meditation.

"Abide in me, and I in you. As the branch cannot bear fruit by itself, unless it abides in the vine, neither can you, unless you abide in me."
John 15:4 (ESV)

2. *Tithing:* There is one place in scripture where God tells us to test Him. He asks us to give one tenth of our income to Him, and He adds a powerful promise as a result. Sometimes you may feel you can't afford to tithe, but try it and see God come through on His promises!

"Bring all the tithe into the storehouse, that there may be food in My house. Try Me now on this," says the Lord of hosts, "If I will not open for you the windows of heaven and pour out for you such blessing that there will not be room enough to receive it."
Malachi 3:10 (NKJV)

3. *Charitable Giving:* Jesus tells us clearly that we are to be about His business of taking care of those who do not have. Whether it be giving financially, giving clothing or food, or standing up for those who cannot stand up for themselves.

"Learn to do right; seek justice. Defend the oppressed. Take up the cause of the fatherless; plead the case of the widow."
Isaiah 1:17 (NIV)

"Suppose a brother or a sister is without clothes and food. If one of you says to them, 'Go in peace; keep warm and well fed,' but does nothing about their physical needs, what good is it?"
James 2:15-16 (NIV)

"No one should seek their own good, but the good of others."
1 Corinthians 10:24 (NIV)

4. *Volunteering:* Sometimes we don't have the resources to give, but we can give of our time. Step aside from taking care of your personal needs for a designated time each week and give of your time. Shift your focus from self to others.

Giving our time to others becomes a balancing factor in our lives. We have already started loving ourselves and believing we matter, which is essential to taking care of ourselves. Now it is time to schedule a few hours of giving our time to others, which will keep us from becoming self-enamored. It is a result of God healing us. It is healthy giving.

Ask the Lord who you need to give to, and what you need to give.

The Bible tells us it so better to give than to receive. Acts 20:35 (ASV) says, "In all things I gave you an example, that so laboring you ought to help the weak, and to remember the words of the Lord Jesus, that He himself said, 'It is more blessed to give than to receive.'"

Psalm 37:4 (AMP) tells us to, "Take delight in the Lord, and He will give you the desires of your heart."

Imagine! When we give our heart to God, He gives us the desires of our hearts! When God plants and grows desires in our hearts, He will fulfill those desires. Our God, the Ultimate Giver, is always giving. We can never out-give the Lord.

Once again, science proves giving creates joy and improves health. An article in the April 2014 issue of *Psychology Today* reported that neurochemicals (dopamine, serotonin, and oxytocin) increase through the act of giving. Giving also boosts your mood, which counteracts the effects of the stress hormone cortisol and counters high levels of oxytocin.

May you continue to give yourself to God so that you may live an abundant life!

"You can give without loving,
but you cannot love without giving."
Amy Carmichael

Empowering a Billion Women
The Art of Giving

Ingrid Vanderveldt

THERE IS
ALWAYS
HOPE

Wow! I was quiet as I listened to the Glambition Radio interview with Ali Brown. The broadcast lingered in my heart and transformed into an increasing intensity, which compelled me to find Ingrid and ask her to share her story with me.

Since I found her, we have embarked on a journey of mentoring, friendship and prayer-partnering. God used Ingrid to expand my dreams, step into my vision with courage, and learn essential business skills I didn't even know I needed.

Ingrid brought with her a global sisterhood of women I desperately longed for, as she is true to her call of Empowering a Billion Women. There is so much to learn from and through this petite, kind, gentle, yet fiery red-head.

• • •

My life's goal is to empower a billion women across the world! It's been quite the journey to work toward this goal. As Dell's first Entrepreneur in Residence (EIR), I oversaw entrepreneurial initiatives worldwide and built a $250 million business segment.

I sit on the United Nations Foundation Global Entrepreneurs Council Board, am a Managing Partner of Dell Capital, and Co-founder of the Billionaires Girls

Club and EBW2020—Empowering a Billion Women by 2020.

Possibility, big vision and fighting against the odds are all part of my DNA. In third grade, my parents received a call from the principal's office informing them I had a learning disability, and that I was failing third grade. In his words, he said, "I was retarded."

My parents refused to accept the assessment and moved me to a different school where I'd have more personal attention. The other kids teased me, but I chose to believe I was special. Later, my parents discovered I had poor hearing, and once that was addressed my learning soared.

I earned a Master's degree from SCAD (Savannah College of Art and Design) and a Masters in Business from McCombs School of Business at the University of Texas. My experiences at SCAD propelled me into orbit for my global work. I won a scholarship, and at age 21 ran for National Office to become the National Director of AIAS (The American Institute for Architecture Students), where I sat in board meetings with politicians, community leaders, and architects. Feeling desperately inexperienced, I decided to pursue a business law degree to understand what the other board members and community leaders were talking about.

I discovered I loved business and started various businesses, some exceedingly successful and others failures. At one point, during my low time, I lost everything. I was homeless and too embarrassed to tell anyone. I lived in my car until an angel of a friend took me in. I curled up in bed for days, depressed.

I was at rock bottom, and I knew I needed to accept where I was and move forward to whatever was ahead. I had to accept the experience as a learning gift from God. I chose to see it as His gift to me, as an opportunity for me to reconnect with my soul, and to surrender my life to His service.

Turning to God made the decision to follow the path of hope easy. It's simple: just ask for help, then walk through all that follows. It's a process where I must show up and do the work. I could give in to the negative energy, or follow the path of love and hope to a better future.

I was raised to believe marriage was for life. For the longest time, it seemed painful relationships plagued me. I was engaged once and loved the man more than words could describe, yet it ended in betrayal. I slowly but surely saw the mental abuse I was experiencing, and just as I thought I was losing my mind, God stepped in! I heard His voice as clear as day, "Leave, leave, leave!" I finally did go, but it took another year to find myself again. Through that relational experience, I discovered authenticity and integrity were all that truly mattered in life.

God continued to mold my character through diverse experiences. I went through tough spots that were difficult to bounce back from, but God deepened my fearless attitude to help me survive through it all. I became comfortable with being uncomfortable.

My desire for global outreach continued to grow, as I knew I could make a lasting impact. An early investor once told me, "Ingrid, you don't need to wait till you're a millionaire. Start thinking back. What has your journey been like? What can you give back today? If you're struggling for cash, how can you help give a little bit of time to help make a difference?"

I believed I could make a difference and was determined to be open, and learn to ask. My belief led me to finally make the decision to hand my life over 100 percent to God's plan.

In 2011 and 2012, a significant shift occurred in my life. I was driving on a country road outside of Dallas, and I prayed, "What do You want me to do today?"

I heard an answer.

"You have done it all. You've achieved much yourself. Now, focus on empowering women by 2020."

I had to ask myself, "Is this my ego?"

"No, it's My asking," God responded.

I made the agreement: "I will Empower a Billion Women by the year 2020."

Very quickly, my entire life changed to focus and move toward my goal. I had to open up and put my ego aside. I had to understand the way God created me to reach people, and how He works, to realize His vision through me. It became apparent that the things I do the best fall into the categories of business, media, and policy initiatives. These were my areas of strength I had to focus on.

I knew I needed to partner with large companies to reach my goal. Dell was the number one technology company for entrepreneurs, and I knew I could reach women through technology. With Dell, I ultimately reached out and connected with women, and men, globally.

When I first met with Dell leadership about the opportunity, I was scared. (I mean, what was I even ASKING of Dell?) But I went anyway. I was at the right place, at the right time. Dell was investing in women entrepreneurs. My vision to achieve the goal to empower women merged with Dell's vision. It was evident we had to put a mobile device into the hands of every woman and to provide her with financial literacy and mentoring.

Mobile devices were the key. What if they were Dell products?

The meeting led to a contract with Dell to become the first Entrepreneur-in-Residence. I drove probability for them, kept costs down, mitigated risks, and served their needs. Through my experience with Dell, I learned if you want to create a relationship with a company to help you go where you want to go, ask them: "How can I be of service to help you reach your goals?" I have since used the same thought process to secure all of my most critical relationships.

It is powerful to see the varied aspects of my life stories come together to form my purpose. My father is from Holland, and his whole family is entrepreneurial. On my mother's side, it's all doctors and nurses. Becoming an entrepreneur and capitalist seemed natural as I began creating opportunities for myself, and my family.

As a child growing up, I thought I would be a missionary, living a life of serving others, and now, globally, I serve through business to create this space for us all to rise together. It comes from a complete place of service and giving that I help others live up to their fullest potential. Giving is my key recipe for success.

The vision and core business strategy of EBW2020 is to work companies for long-term success. We aim to be Angel Investors for young tech businesses and accomplish philanthropy work by funding women's businesses in developing countries.

We are committed to bringing our expertise as we help partners and clients build meaningful business relationships with each other. EBW2020 is a platform to provide educational opportunities, empower women with leadership skills, share knowledge, connect with each other, and provide access to resources and capital.

I learned that through giving, we receive in completely unexpected ways. Once I went into 100 percent service, the United Nations heard of the work I was doing with Dell. They knew it was important to me to work on a policy about the issues women and girls face.

I was humbled when the UN asked me to sit on the Foundation Global Entrepreneurship Council, which focuses on global issues. It felt as if God gave me the gift of everything I'd asked for on a silver platter, after having asked Him how He could use my experiences and gifts to make a difference in the lives of women worldwide.

Through the United Nations platform, I could focus on policy issues involving women and girls around the world. Now, I'm also on the Board of the Girl-Up Initiative through the UN Foundation, which connects girls in the United States to girls in developing countries. I thank God every day for the opportunity.

I truly believe if we are going to turn around our global economy, it will not happen with the large companies. It will be the entrepreneurs and small business owners who will do it; it will be the women who will do it. This women-centered philosophy is the foundation for all of the work I am blessed to have done and continue to do.

Love is where purpose-filled living starts. Giving flows from love. I am very honored to live a life of service. We all have the opportunity to dream big and use our talents. What an extraordinary journey occurs when we do!

• • •

To find out more about Empowering a Billion Women by 2020 (EBW2020), to join an EBW Chapter, attend an EBW Event or Retreat, or learn more about the Empowerment programs visit: EBW2020.com

"Find your calling.
Dream big.
Seek help.
Impact the world."
Ingrid Vanderveldt

For Prayerful Application

Anytime you go out to live the life you are called to, it is scary and lonely. It all comes down to you. Can you trust God enough to take the first step to start the forward momentum? Once you take the first step, the resources, the people, and everything you need begins to come together. It's usually harder than you thought and the path is different than you imagined. Keep taking baby steps! You will face an important decision: stay where you are, or choose to believe and move forward.

"Fear not, for I am with you; Be not dismayed, for I am your God. I will strengthen you, Yes, I will help you, I will uphold you with My righteous right hand."
Isaiah 41:10 (NKJV)

"If any of you lacks wisdom, you should ask God, who gives generously to all without finding fault, and it will be given to you."
James 1:5 (NIV)

"I will instruct you and teach you in the way you should go; I will counsel you with my loving eye on you."
Psalm 32:8 (NIV)

Find a mentor. Do you have wise counsel? Someone bigger than you who has been where you're going?

"A wise man will hear and increase in learning,
and a man of understanding will acquire wise counsel."
Proverbs 1:5 (NASB)

Find a support group of five women who believe in you, stretch you, encourage you, and hold you accountable.

"Where there is no guidance the people fall,
but in abundance of counselors there is victory."
Proverbs 11:14 (NASB)

"Where there is no counsel the people fail,
but in multitude of counselors there is safety."
Proverbs 19:20 (NKJV)

Proactive Listening & Giving Back

The Art of Giving

Natalie Phillips

THERE IS
ALWAYS
HOPE

Natalie's warmth, joy, and energy touch me, whether in person, on the phone, or in a photo. We met at Empowering Billion Women's first event, and stayed connected on Facebook. We embarked on the journey together as Chapter Leaders for EBW 2020, and now we're soul sisters.

Sharing stories bound our hearts together. Natalie is an authentic, strong, smart, business woman, mom, and spouse. She is one who empowers and hears the cry of the hearts around her.

• • •

It almost seemed I lived the perfect life growing up—almost. I grew up in Hawaii and attended a Christian school where I excelled in sports, sang in vocal ensembles and school musicals, and loved my advanced placement math and science classes. My heritage is Hawaiian, Chinese, and Christian.

I identified as a jock who ran with the popular crowd. I always tried to fit in, dated only certain people and wore popular clothing styles. By my senior year in high school, I was tired of following the crowd.

"Enough!" I finally said to myself. "I want to do what I want to do!"

My senior year became the best year of my high school experience. I widened my circle, choosing to be friends with a variety of people. I mixed and mingled with the academics, jocks, and drama crowd. I continued to sing, and my class voted me as the Student Body Vice President.

I also joined what was called the "Servants Group," where I learned more about God and applying His Word to my life. I learned to make a difference by giving of myself. During the lunch hour, I no longer rushed off campus to hang out with the "cool kids" and make bad decisions. Instead, I spent my time building relationships.

Unfortunately, in college I slam-dunked my wise choices! I was seventeen my freshman year in Colorado, and I went crazy. Once again, I felt I needed to look good and hang out with what appeared to be the popular crowd, attend house parties, and sneak into bars using a fake ID. Thank goodness, God protected me during that time. I came to my senses my sophomore year and once again made choices that were good for my heart.

I ended up switching majors a few times. God guided me through my mom's suggestions, and I began to consider Speech Pathology and Audiology as a career. The more I researched about the field, the more I loved it. I dove right in and was still able to graduate on time.

Upon entering graduate school back in Hawaii, I had to decide between speech and audiology. I had friends who couldn't hear, and my thoughts immediately went to them. I chose to pursue a degree in audiology—the study of hearing and treating people with hearing loss.

I met my husband, Jason, in Colorado where we both refereed for college basketball. We continued dating after I went back to Hawaii for grad school, and he went on to his first job in South Dakota with the Continental Basketball Association. The long-distance relationship was difficult for both of us, so after one semester he quit his job and moved to Hawaii. Once I completed my Master's degree, we married. After my clinical fellowship, he wanted to pursue his Master's degree, so we moved to Texas.

That move was beginning of our nomad lifestyle. We knew our life together was not going to be "typical." Slowly, we started understanding God was protecting us and preparing us to be more for Him.

Shortly after our move, loneliness settled into my heart. I had a great need to feel I belonged as a wife, an Audiologist, and a person. No one seemed to understand our situation and why we weren't staying put, buying a house, and having children now that we were married.

Reflecting on my experience growing up, I often felt bad about never really having a best friend. I always felt I was odd or weird because I didn't have one special friend, even though I had a lot of friends. Perhaps that's why I tried so hard to be popular when I was younger, and why I struggled with loneliness.

Once again, Mom's words of wisdom reached into my lonely place in Texas as she suggested we find a church and begin making friends. We followed her advice and the church we attended was a different kind of church than I had ever attended. There were no musical instruments; the singing was a cappella.

The voices touched my heart, and I knew almost immediately as we walked through the door that it was the church where we belonged. It is remarkable how sound and hearing constantly beckon me, and how God always weaves sound into my choices.

The church was exactly what we needed. They had a young marrieds group we hung out with all the time. We had fun eating together, playing games, chatting, traveling, serving other families, and studying God's Word. I loved how we accepted each other with our quirks, our strengths, and our love for our spouses and each other.

I could be myself, and people loved me for it! Mom was right! I have learned such a great lesson from our church and from that first move. Now, one of the first things I do upon arrival at a new place is to go out and make friends!

I now see my ability to connect with many people, as opposed to having just one special best friend, as a strength. With every move, I don't have to grieve the loss of one close relationship, and I can repeatedly connect to others in ever-changing environments.

I learned to find commonalities between myself and others and automatically make connections. I care about everyone I meet, and I want to learn from as many people as I can in this lifetime. I'm the same way with my patients. I truly want to know about their lives, not just their hearing loss or needs.

Approximately a year and a half later, as Jason was finishing up his Master's degree in Texas, we decided to move to the West Coast to be halfway between both of our families. I accepted a job offer in Southern California from the University of California Irvine Medical Center. They desperately needed an Audiologist.

Jason was selected for an internship in Northern California with the San Francisco 49ers, which he gave up for me. We moved to Southern California, and I began to work on my career, which fully blossomed. After a few years, I joined a private medical practice in Orange County, the local go-to practice. It was everything I could have dreamed.

Meanwhile, Jason struggled. He wanted to be a Strength and Conditioning Coach, but the doors were not opening. He held a number of odd jobs, including working as a security guard and football coach at a high school. Finally, he received a position as an Assistant Strength and Conditioning Coach at the University of California in Irving. The University didn't have a football program, which was a major part of his passion. Another low point was that the University paid very low wages, and I became the major breadwinner. His job was hard on us and our marriage.

Thankfully, we joined a church. It was the largest church I have ever been in—Saddleback Community Church. I sang in the gospel choir, and we joined a small group, which held us accountable. What a blessing!

Before we knew it, Jason received a call from the San Diego Chargers. "We'd love you to come and work for the summer; however, there's no guarantee about a job in the fall." Graciously, the University of California in Irvine said they would hold his job for him to allow him the experience working with the Chargers. Every day that summer, he drove the one-and-a-half-hour commute.

We had been married for about seven years, and the proverbial "seven-year itch" brought some hard times in our marriage. I recall asking him one night, "Do you even love me?" He couldn't answer, and my heart broke.

I am so thankful for our church small group that encouraged us to go to marriage counseling. We went, sheepishly and embarrassed. It was tough and hard. Thankfully, we made it through. We realized we were both equally important. I stopped trying to control the family by the fact that I excelled in my job and was the principal breadwinner. The spouse with the highest income did not determine the future. I acknowledged how difficult my husband's career struggle was on his ego. I had to learn to see and empathize with his needs. I learned a lot.

The next summer the Chargers called Jason to return to San Diego for another summer internship. This time, however, UC Irvine said they wouldn't hold his job.

"You need to go," I said, supportively. "We'll figure it out." I knew he needed to love his job. He gave up the NFL position for me back when we moved to Southern California, and now it was his turn to pursue his dreams and for me to sacrifice.

Very shortly after we stepped out in faith, God delivered. Jason received a full-time position as an Assistant Strength Coach at Oregon State University.

He had to move up north the following week! My heart ached as I left my "dream job." A few months later, I found out I was pregnant. I was now in Oregon, had no job, didn't feel well from the pregnancy, lived in a small apartment, and had no friends.

It was difficult searching for fulfillment in the midst of the constant ebb and flow of transitioning to a new location. As a professional, it was challenging knowing I could have a private practice, which I desperately wanted if we had not moved. I wanted to experience the pride of establishing a practice, watching it grow, and achieving major success. I felt torn between what I wanted and who I "had" to be.

I was angry at my situation, but God reminded me I knew how to find work, make friends, select a church, and buy a house. The adjustment cycle came and went so fast, before I knew it we were off to Seattle as my husband accepted yet another new position as he grew in his career.

Our son was 14-months-old, and I was working four days a week at a clinic when I became pregnant with my daughter. Once again, the volatility of Jason's career erupted, and his new job ended. He collected unemployment for three months and became "daddy daycare" for us to make ends meet. There were days where I thought, "This can't be the life God prepared us for." Then the call came from Colorado State University; moving there was like going home for us!

Along the way, not only had I learned to be gracious toward my husband as he pursued his dreams, but he also started making different choices for our family. He began taking us into consideration. He turned down a seemingly great, yet volatile position at the university for a more stable one and became the Head Strength and Conditioning Coach of Olympic Sports, which included all sports at the University except for his favorite, football! He finally had his own staff, created his own environment, and earned more money.

We have now lived in Fort Collins, Colorado for over seven years. Looking back, it was time for my husband's career to take off when it did. When we both decided to give to each other and our family, our lives started working out. I believe God rewarded us for choosing to prioritize our commitment to our family, our marriage, and one another.

As my life finally found a measure of stability, I realized I couldn't just talk the talk, but I had to walk the walk. I have to show up for my husband to show support for his position, his gifts, and his passion. He started working with the University men's basketball and women's volleyball teams, which were the two sports I played and loved to watch. I finally decided to show up as a wife and bring the family to games. It made such a difference. It also helped the athletes view him as a part of a family, which was a necessary safeguard for our marriage—a lesson I learned from my parents who divorced after over 35 years of marriage.

In my thirties, I learned about my dad's double life and his affairs. The woman he was involved with during my high school and college years was always present in his life, but we did not know it. I began to notice my mom wasn't interested in my dad's work environment or some of his interests. She did not show up for him, but there was someone who did. Ultimately, the affair ended, but the pattern did not stop.

I was angry when the truth about my dad came out. Although counseling worked for my husband and me, it wasn't an option for my parents. Growing up, my family looked perfect from the outside. We always attended church and went to Christian schools. My parents taught Sunday school and lead youth groups. Our family was not what people assumed us to be.

When the imperfections came to the surface, it was difficult for me to walk out my faith and keep my head high. I was consumed with shame. I initially coped by shutting my dad out and trying to support my mom, as everyone seemed to be doing. Even though I did it myself, a part of me was upset that so many people surrounded my mom with support while at the same time let my dad go.

Dad continued to hurt me as I watched him spend very little time with our family while spending quality time with "her."

"I'm going to marry her. Natalie, please come to the wedding." Dad asked me.

I didn't want to be involved. It was hard for me. My sister reminded me that I always have a choice. I can choose who I want in my life and who I don't. Whatever I chose, I would have to live with it as it was my decision.

He was my dad. I had to go. I would keep it together and go to the wedding to support him.

It was tough going to the wedding. I sat there listening to people talk about how dad and the new woman were meant to be, and that God brought them together.

All I could think was, "You all know he was married during all this, right?"

As I was leaving the wedding festivities, my dad walked me to the car saying. "I'm so glad you were able to come out," he said as he started crying.

Finally, I was able to say something and mean it. "I am glad to see you happy, Dad."

The stress of my parent's divorce and my dad's remarriage impacted my health and tipped me over the edge. I was thirty pounds overweight and developed medical conditions that would have me on medication for the rest of my life if I did not choose to fight for my health.

I had to take care of my physical and emotional health. My stepmom worked hard to build our relationship, and a significant part of my healing process was thankfulness to have my dad back in my life.

Nine months later, my phone rang. The caller ID showed my dad's number.

"Hey, Dad! What's up?" I asked.

But it wasn't my dad; it was my stepbrother. "Natalie, so sorry to tell you, your dad passed away suddenly today. He had a heart attack."

It hadn't even been a year since the wedding. I was so grateful I let Dad back in my life, and that God compelled me to forgive and to give love and time to him.

My mom and dad's story was a gift that taught me the essential give-and-take needed for a successful marriage. My husband and I know the importance of being present in each other's lives, as well as in our children's lives. We need to be involved with every member of our family. It's a constant giving, one to the other.

To be happy, both my husband and I must pursue our individual passions and callings. We all know basketball season is Dad's time to focus on the team. I stay home, while he jet-sets around with the team. When he's back home, I can attend to my purpose, working with other entrepreneurial women and going on mission trips with the Starkey Hearing Foundation to take the gift of hearing to less privileged people.

Whenever the kids need to be picked up or dropped off at activities, we share the responsibility. We show each other mutual respect and know that one career or job position is not more important than the other.

We serve the student-athletes together as a family team. On occasion, we welcome them into our home for a meal, conversation, and a family away from home. I spend time with coaches and athletes as I listen to their dreams and stories. I help connect them to walk in purpose and to focus on core life principles.

Through my journey, I not only learned the steps I needed to navigate change, marriage, and relationships successfully, I also learned valuable business lessons. Each stopping place in my career taught me something to make me more marketable in my profession. I learned how to create spreadsheets, how to calculate my salary, how to walk confidently into a practice to assess their needs, to know how to help them build their resources, and ultimately how to create profit and revenue.

With each position I took, I became more confident in my ability to negotiate and make promises I could deliver. With every move, the best I could say to my employer was, "You have me for three to five years, and here is what I can do for you while I am here." It always amazed me that starting off on the right foot by being truthful created a sense of trust and understanding moving forward.

At one point, I thought about giving up audiology. I had to assess what I loved and realized I love working with patients and helping them with their hearing. I loved the fantastic Christian practice I worked in where I set my schedule.

One of my treasured friends told me, "You know you have a bigger calling. You cannot be concerned with owning a private practice." I knew she was right. I felt a peace about letting go of my dream for a private practice. God often speaks through people and always at the right time.

I am blessed to use my life experiences to help others. To truly make a difference in someone's life, you can't be afraid to share your story and to be thankful for what God has allowed you to live and learn. Being authentic connects people. I have learned there's no time to be fake. Learn the lessons, learn them quick, and be open to sharing.

Sometimes it isn't easy to be vulnerable. The negative behavior and comments of others can impact me if I let them. Not even a year ago, people I thought were friends said some very hurtful things to me.

"You are not *that* special; you don't even have your own business. Why would people be interested in you? You know, you are only where you are because I helped you get there. I don't see you running a business. You know, people really don't care about you, so just move on."

I had to learn to pull the knife out of my heart and keep pushing forward. I had to learn to discern who was good for me and who wasn't, to move people out of my inner circle if needed, and to know the right time to make changes. I had to learn to ignore the noise from the people who merely draw on my energy and to make room to give my fullest attention to the people God wanted me to help.

God gave me a story to share about how I have overcome many obstacles. I can never allow other people to deter me from what I am called to do. I may not know fully what all I will do in my life and calling, but will I continue to listen and be obedient. I will take the opportunities God places in my path.

I love working with women and being a part of Empowering a Billion Women by 2020—EBW2020. The more I give, the more I learn, and the more my confidence grows. I can see how my work as an Audiologist transitioned from focusing on physical hearing to focusing on heartfelt soul-hearing. I love active listening, communication through social media, and the endless necessity of creating environments where women can connect. I am excited and energized for all that lies ahead knowing I can never out-give God! Woohoo!

• • •

To connect with Natalie, email her at dr.nphillips@hotmail.com or on Twitter @AudioDrPhillips.

For Prayerful Application

1. Do you practice the skill of give-and-take in your marriage or primary relationships? Do you respect that each person has "their" season?

"But if anyone does not provide for his relatives,
and especially for members of his household,
he has denied the faith and is worse than an unbeliever."
1 Timothy 5:8 (ESV)

2. Can you give of yourself and your time to be a shoulder for someone to lean on when they need you, even when they hurt you, themselves and others?

"Brothers, if anyone is caught in any transgression,
you who are spiritual should restore him in a spirit of
gentleness. Keep watch on yourself, lest you too be tempted.
Bear one another's burdens, and so fulfill the law of Christ.
For if anyone thinks he is something, when he is nothing, he
deceives himself. But let each one test his own work, and then
his reason to boast will be in himself alone and not in his
neighbor. For each will have to bear his own load."
Galatians 6:1-5 (ESV)

3. Do you focus on developing a healthy core group that holds you accountable?

"And let us consider how to stir up one another to love and good works, not neglecting to meet together, as is the habit of some, but encouraging one another, and all the more as you see the Day drawing near."
Hebrews 10:24, 25 (ESV)

"The measure of a life, after all, is not its duration, but its donation."
Corrie Ten Boom

Coming Full Circle
The Art of Giving

Regeanie Corona

THERE IS
ALWAYS
HOPE

We clasped hands in the foyer at the United Nations, our eyes looking deeply into each other's heart. It was a Holy moment. We prayed. God came into the present, assuring us of the call for the future. Later that day, after the tour, Regeanie said she had experienced what she calls kisses from heaven, when God takes a moment and gives a glimpse of destiny. Tearfully, she said she heard Him say, "My promise to you is, you are called to the nations."

Now we marvel, not even a year later, as we see God unfold His plan. It all started with Regeanie surrendering her life, her time, and her resources in obedience to Him.

• • •

I had two wonderful, loving parents who were not perfect. My dad was a social alcoholic; a most lovable man who validated me and assured me I was valuable and loved. His love was a key component of establishing my identity in my formative years and remains at the core of who I am today. My mom was the disciplined one who walked steadily; she gave me a stable foundation of faith and made sure I attended church every week.

I gave my life to Jesus when I was twelve and had tremendous faith. God blessed me with a prophetic gifting, and I would see things in my spirit I couldn't explain. The visions I would have strengthened my faith, and I knew I was going to do something great one day. I didn't know what exactly I would do, but I confidently shared my calling with my mother who smiled and nodded at my words.

When God showed me a vision, it was as if He were putting money into a bank account, and giving me a promise it would begin to grow. I saw how God delegated power and authority to us as human beings. As a child, I intuitively understood the power of my words. When I spoke kind words, I was able to lift others up. Equally so, I could tear people down with my words. God began to use me at a young age to edify others.

Growing up, I also experienced the painful power of words. I was a multi-racial child, uncommon in the inner city where I grew up. Many of my peers bullied me and challenged my identity. I didn't understand why they teased me and didn't know how to handle it. In my heart, I struggled to love myself. I hated my hair and the color of my skin. I projected a "tough girl" exterior.

God was faithful to me, but I was not obedient to Him. Rebellion entered my life when I started dating at age 15. I gave up my virginity in an attempt validate who I was as a person. I did not lean on Jesus but instead grasped at the things of the world. My human desires outweighed my spiritual commitment.

At 19, I decided to marry even though I knew the choice was not God's destiny for me. I knowingly walked straight into an abusive relationship. He was verbally abusive, insecure, and dominated my life. Occasionally, he would even physically abuse me. I gave up a four-year scholarship to college and spent 12 years in a bad relationship.

I struggled to survive spiritually instead of growing into the woman I was meant to be. I dimmed my light so that my husband would not feel as insecure. The more insecure he felt, the worse the verbal or physical abuse was for me. I tried to be the wife God wanted me to be, but I had no power in the relationship.

I turned my attention to building my career. I worked and established myself in the Information Technology industry. Twelve years into my marriage, I discovered my husband had a six-year-old child. He had lied to me for at least half of our marriage. I tried to forgive and rebuild the relationship with unconditional love. But my husband couldn't understand or reciprocate unconditional love. Instead, he gave an unhealthy, toxic love, and never worked on the relationship. The marriage ended.

I was 31 when my dear father died. It was a pivotal point in my life, and God used the pain to strengthen me. Two days after his death, I learned I was adopted. I had never paused to consider why I was so fair-skinned, yet my parents were both African-American. By the grace of God, the knowledge of truth came as a moment of relief. Finally, my world seemed to make sense. My heart flooded with love and curiosity. I felt so loved to know my loving family chose to take me in as their own.

If it were not for God's grace, I could have experienced bitterness, anger, and possibly even hate at the realization that I was adopted. Oh, but the grace of God! He showers us with peace and thanks when we allow Him into our lives and our hearts.

I went back to school and started the process of becoming who God made me to be. My career began to flourish amidst the process of divorce and rebuilding my life as a single woman. Apparently, I hadn't learned all my lessons. I became romantically involved with a friend I worked with. I wasn't ready for another marriage, but I was fearful of being alone. I still had issues I continued to ignore; namely, searching for love, security, and affirmation externally instead of building from within with God's love. Once again, I made a commitment to marry knowing it was not what God wanted from me.

In the eleventh year of my second marriage, my mom became terminally ill with cancer. The doctors said she had a mere two weeks to live. I took a break from working at my training and development company and became her caregiver.

We had the most amazing three weeks together. For the first time, we spoke intimately and bonded deeply. Her last words to me were, "God misses you and wants you back. He wants your attention. You absolutely need Him. Promise me you will make your relationship with the Lord a priority in your life again."

I admitted I had allowed my husband, who was not a believer, to influence me to follow his ways. I still had faith, but I did not have a strong relationship with Jesus. Mom's final sweet gift to me was turning my eyes back to Jesus.

When she passed, I felt at such a loss. We were finally close, and now I couldn't go back to get more of her. I mourned her in a way I had not mourned my dad.

Soon after my mom passed, I became pregnant with my daughter. I had wanted children for such a long time, and the baby was a kiss from God. My daughter was a heaven-sent gift to ease the pain in my heart.

Still, it was a challenging time. Doctors ordered me on bed rest and said the baby would have physical and mental challenges. The doctor wanted me to have an amniosynthesis, an amniotic fluid test to confirm any potential chromosome defects. I decided against the test, as I felt it could harm my precarious pregnancy even more. I knew in my Spirit my child was going to be okay.

In those days, it was rare to have access to a 3D ultrasound, but God made a way, and we were able to confirm my baby's health. She was born healthy and happy. I was in love, enamored.

Time passed, and the void from losing my mother me grew inside of me again. I felt empty. I didn't know what to do or how to make it better.

I became pregnant again, but I lost the baby at five and a half months. I thought I was finished having kids, but two months later I was pregnant again. I went through another difficult pregnancy, but, thankfully, my son was born healthy.

When the children were one and three, the gap between my husband and me widened. I yearned for a life partner with whom I could bond. Three years later, I made the hardest decision of my life. I separated from my husband, the father of my children, and became a single parent.

I continued to validate myself through my external life: building my career, perfectionism, and a non-stop drive forward. One day, I felt God begin to speak. He was reaching for my attention. I knew in my spirit God was saying, "I need to use you, but I can't use you as you are. You have to be willing to go through a heart change to live in your destiny."

I wrote a list of what needed to change in my life: pride, self-righteousness, vanity and lack of trust were at the top of the list. At first, I did not want to own responsibility for my sin. I argued with God. I didn't want to see the reality of the person God was showing me in the mirror.

Finally, I stepped back and recounted my life. Gracefully, God allowed me to see exactly what He was referring to. At that moment, I said, "Do whatever you have to do. No matter how painful it is. I will walk through the fire. I give you my all." It was the beginning of my brokenness, a milestone. I saw who I was and what needed to change. Spiritually, it was a difficult and challenging time, yet God was there guiding, unfolding, and teaching.

Before my divorce, I was earning a six-figure income. Due to complexities with the divorce, I went broke. I didn't know if I could pay my bills from month to month. Even though I felt more connected to God, I still felt empty and alone in my struggles.

I went back to church and began to pray and walk in the faith God had given me when I was a child. I started to learn how to love myself and to see God's love for me. Once I started understanding His love, I gained the ability to love other people. It took another two years of God breaking me down and rebuilding me from the heart level. I let go and let God do the work in me. Finally, He fully exchanged my heart for His.

Before, I had always focused on what was going on with me and my struggles. As God did His work, I no longer focused on me. I realized my destiny, even my very existence, was not about me. I was not alive to please myself but to share the story of my journey. God can use each experience to help, encourage, motivate, and inspire others. I learned to get up every day with a grateful and joyful heart and outlook, no matter what. Each day was a gift from the Lord.

At age 12, God had already given me everything I needed. The power was inside of me, but I didn't know how to access it. In 2011, my journey came full circle, and I began tapping into my true inheritance and learning how to use it. I started walking with conviction and purpose.

God called me to help young people and women find, stand, and work boldly in their purpose. He has called me to share my faith unapologetically. I am committed to answering His call wherever I go. If I can inspire anyone through sharing a part of my journey, I will. My faith has brought me to where I am today. I do not want to take my treasure to the grave with me; I must liberally share it.

On Good Friday, 2013, I married God's choice of a husband for me. We committed our vows to keep God first, both individually and as a couple. We promised that we each would keep God first, then family, then self.

At first, I was embarrassed to admit I was in my third marriage. I was disobedient twice in my life, but God's grace took all I did in disobedience and used it for His incredible good. I am now happier than I've ever been! It is not all perfect, but whatever happens, we pray, look to the Lord, and His Word. We go to the Power greater we are.

I have learned obedience to God is what allows me to stand in grace and righteousness, and to stay full of peace and joy in the midst of any storm. God has transformed my life. He has called me to spread the Gospel, and share His Word.

He has called me to be love and light in the world. Finally, I'm at peace even if people hate me. I have learned to use fear as fuel for my fire. When I wake up in the morning, the Holy Spirit speaks to my spirit and guides me to obedience. He provides and blesses. In His strength, I can step into my calling daily to love everyone and relentlessly share the joy and light Jesus gives me.

• • •

To learn more about Regeanie and the work she does, visit AdvanceTheSeed.org, Abizstrategies.com, or Regeanie.com.

Or email her at rcorona@tnsmconsulting.com.

"Stay active. Read the Word.
Worship with other believers.
Continue to give. Keep learning and growing.
Your faith will be unleashed!"
Joyce Meyers

For Prayerful Application

1. Have you allowed the Holy Spirit to break you down and build you up His way?

"Truly, truly, I say to you, unless a grain of wheat
falls into the earth and dies, it remains alone;
but if it dies, it bears much fruit."
John 12:24 (NASB)

2. Will you allow the Lord to unpack your stories of the past, heal you, refine you, and remove what doesn't belong so you can be all He created you to be?

"I am the true vine, and my Father is the gardener.
He cuts off every branch in me that bears no fruit,
while every branch that does bear fruit he prunes
so that it will be even more fruitful."
John 15:1-2 (NIV)

3. Can you commit to spending time in God's Word, in prayer and being obedient to His tasks of giving your love as He designed for you?

"You are already clean because of the word I have spoken to you. Remain in me, as I also remain in you. No branch can bear fruit by itself; it must remain in the vine. Neither can you bear fruit unless you remain in me. I am the vine; you are the branches.

If you remain in me and I in you, you will bear much fruit; apart from me you can do nothing. If you do not remain in me, you are like a branch that is thrown away and withers; such branches are picked up, thrown into the fire and burned. If you remain in me and my words remain in you, ask whatever you wish, and it will be done for you. This is to my Father's glory, that you bear much fruit, showing yourselves to be my disciples. As the Father has loved me, so have I loved you. Now remain in my love. If you keep my commands, you will remain in my love, just as I have kept my Father's commands and remain in his love. I have told you this so that my joy may be in you and that your joy may be complete. My command is this: Love each other as I have loved you."
John 15:3-12 (NIV)

CONCLUSION

A Story Exemplifying all 5 Essential Life Skills

A Mad-Thing Into A Glad-Thing

Cherie Matthews

THERE IS
ALWAYS
HOPE

Her black hair, sparkling eyes, and huge smile drew me in. Then she spoke. The entire group of women riveted as we sat sipping drinks alongside the San Antonio River Walk. Her voice captivated us. Each time she spoke at EBW 2020 Millionaire's Retreat, she gave a little of herself and made a difference. She encouraged and mentored us.

The year that followed, she unexpectedly stepped into my life, giving guidance, and pouring into my work. Each time we interacted was a gift.

Cherie is a giver like no other. Her life epitomizes mastering the 5 Life Skills. Hers is a story of a bad thing happening to a good person, and a journey of rising again. Hers is a story of a woman who let God write His story through her life. He stepped into her darkest moment and used it for a myriad of good.

• • •

I was in trouble. There I lay, throw-up all over my shirt. Tubes coming out of me, my breasts were suddenly gone. I was disfigured.

A snapshot of my early life tells me I had every reason to feel "less than." My dad raised me in Canada from the age of seven on. When I was fifteen, we moved to the United States.

I remember the blessing my architect Dad gave me. He pulled up in his business truck with the name

'Cher Developments LTD' painted on both sides of the truck. I remember saying, "Dad, that's my name on your truck!"

"Get used to seeing your name," he replied. Our bond deepened, as did my confidence in our world of riding around in fast cars, motorcycles, and boats. I even learned to gap a spark plug. Dad didn't play Barbies with me, but we fixed broken things together. In middle school, we went to leadership camps together where we learned to live off the land and scale down mountains.

Before I knew it, my college days had begun. I went into Computer Engineering before the dawn of computers. My goal was to be an employee of IBM. When I interviewed with them, I told them they were the only company I wanted to work for and why.

Their answer, "We have never had an interview like this. You are telling us to hire you."

"Yes, sir!" I said, and they hired me.

I found Jesus and my intention turned toward a purpose. I met Adam, my hubby, at IBM and our life journey began. I started a jail ministry and had our beautiful daughter Ashley and son Adam.

I continued to live my life purposefully. My love of golf and its core values inspired me. I started to dream about teaching kids important life skills through golf.

"Why can't children play golf?" I asked myself.

My dream became a reality and my friend, Benna Call, and I co-pioneered what is known today as the *First Tee National School Program*. We teach 9 Core Values: honesty, integrity, sportsmanship, respect, confidence, responsibility, perseverance, courtesy, and judgment, all the while teaching kids to play golf. We started going into schools and teaching kids; then we began training teachers to teach their students. The *First Tee National School Program* has now reached 10 million kids. Children became my life.

I was a happy person who served God, my family, and my community. I was an organic eater, long distance runner, and was healthy. I had just walked into my house after coming back from a ski trip when I saw the phone message light blinking (those were the days before cell phones).

I had previously been for a check-up and mammogram, and the message was from the radiology department.

"Sorry to inform you, but you have breast cancer." They left the message just like that.

I plunged into research and came up with an action plan. It felt as if I fell into a big black hole, grasping, groping for hope. I was scared, but I knew God had a plan. I knew my work on earth was not done. Before I knew it, we had scheduled a double mastectomy.

Here's where my next life story began.

The night before my surgery, I sat in a chair and had a meltdown. I was alone wondering if God was even with me. It was a knee-jerking cliché when people would say, "You can do all things through Christ that strengthens you."

I was close to God, but I couldn't feel Him. It was the loneliest moment of my life. I whispered a prayer, "I can't feel You anymore. Can't hear you. I'm afraid. What if they open me up and it's everywhere?"

I then felt a weight on my arm. Startled, I looked around. I was very upset and had trouble seeing through my tears, but there was no one there. Then I heard, "I am your High Priest. I will never leave you or forsake you."

It was a promise for my soul. My tears dried up.

After the surgery, I woke up to a very uptight, tired nurse who curtly said, "We need to get you up and get you out."

I looked down at my horrific self, and in desperation, I asked for my lipstick. The pain engulfed me, and I couldn't sit up. I asked for help.

"No more meds for you. You're maxed out. Get dressed."

I couldn't push my arm into my man-shirt and became sick all over the shirt.

The nurse was irritated. "Why did you bring this shirt?" She might as well have rolled her eyes.

"Well, this is my first mastectomy," I answered. "Why didn't you have something for me to go home in so I didn't have to guess and pick the incorrect thing?"

"Women have always suffered in silence," the nurse said. "We don't offer anything for you to go home in. You have a right and left drain stitched into your body." She placed the drains into my hands.

"What should I do with these drains?" I asked.

"We have safety pins for you to pin the tubes to your shirt."

It made me upset to think that a patient with a sprained elbow receives a sling to aid in their recovery, but mastectomy patients do not have any standardized garments to recover in. Surely mastectomy patients matter as much as those with a sprained elbow! I am certain if a man lost his man parts in a battle against cancer, they wouldn't send him home in his wife's skirt with safety pins.

Why is it okay for them to recommend women to bring in an oversized button-down when they have had their breasts removed? IT'S NOT OK!

They sent me home with throw-up on my shirt and body fluid leaking into dreadful tubes for everyone to see. I couldn't even greet my children in a dignified manner as I walked through the door of our house.

I was angry and determined to do something about it. I looked like a science experiment, bent over, ashen, embarrassed that I was a broken person, and still worried about cancer and being around long enough to raise our young children.

I refused to have guests, except for my BFF, because of the way I looked. After a few days, I shuffled into my closet and cried as I looked at my clothes. I had fancy clothes, golf clothes, and motorbike clothes, but none of my clothes gave me hope. I had nothing to help me adapt to my new circumstances.

"This is just too hard," I said.

Women do care about what we look like, even in our toughest battles. I looked terrible. My hair, my pasty face, my mauled body. I was not the same woman.

For ten years, I was silent about my cancer experience, yet the burning voice in my heart screamed out. I vowed to do something about what happens in the horrific days after mastectomy.

"You said you're going to fix it, so fix it. You vowed. You promised," I said, holding myself accountable.

After experiencing the pain and the tube drains, I knew what the hospital recovery wear should have been. I told a friend I had an idea for a standardized garment, but I didn't know how to start. "I am an inventor of ideas and programs, not clothing."

To top that off, I failed home economics at school because I stapled my hem (it seemed more efficient at the time). There had to be a way for me to learn to sew! I watched the Coco Chanel movie three times and learned I could be "a boss of fabric."

Then, I hustled off to the courthouse and filed for a DBA. I started a website, HealInComfort.com. I designed comfortable shirts with four internal pockets to discretely hide medical drains for post-operative surgery.

24 hours later, I received a call from Fox News for an interview. No, I don't have a prototype yet. No, I don't want to talk about my mastectomy. Yes, I will do the interview.

Oh, dear! I need to prepare for TV!

I ran to a sports store and a fabric store. I found a seamstress. I glued pieces of material together and made a prototype for the TV interview. I made it clear to the interviewers that they were to ask me about my idea, but not about my mastectomy.

I quickly learned that God calls us to sacrifice our pride, and then the windows of heaven open up.

The interview began.

"Cherie Matthews has a company HealInComfort. So, Cherie, tell us about your double mastectomy."

Ow! I had to go straight into the storm, right then and there. But the windows of heaven have opened up as a result of me opening up!

Before I knew it, I'd sold my first twenty-five shirts in Austin. Then fifty were gone. Testimonies started pouring in.

"This shirt is my safe blankey. I can hide in this. What a blessing!"

Okay, I'll do a hundred more then I'm done. I'll move on with my life. I prayed for each woman that she might recover in dignity and comfort. Before I knew it, I'd made a thousand more shirts. The business just kept growing and growing.

When you have an idea burning in your heart, and you get on with doing what's asked of you, God's blessings will follow. My spirit, my heart, and my faith are now aligned. I left pride and ego behind me. It's a vulnerable place to be, yet it is so exciting.

There were many days I felt too tired to keep going. It seemed too hard. God reminded me of the story of Jonah. He refused to do what he was called to do, so he was thrown overboard and swallowed by a whale (I believe it was a whale shark that spit Jonah out right in front of the people he was meant to serve, with fish 'ick' all over him).

I didn't want to have a whale spit me out with fish 'ick' on me. I wanted to serve God, so I pressed on. What an amazing journey to see God use my story for good. HealInComfort has reached 10,000 women, and some men. I have been able to send shirts to Nicaragua, where women were doing self-surgeries, becoming infected, and dying. Sending shirts to them was like sending hugs from American sisters saying, "We care about you and you can HealInComfort too."

I have built a "pay-it-forward" system into my business plan by starting an independently run non-profit called, Gifting Care. It's my soul-pay. My end goal is to change the procedural discharge after surgery for all mastectomy patients. I hope one day that each woman who goes through a mastectomy will receive my patented HealInComfort shirt to go home in and to recover in comfort and dignity. Mastectomy patients need more recovery wear than a patient with a sprained elbow!

The crabbiest nurse of nurses ended up being such a HUGE blessing. We can put our hands on our hips and complain about the mud pit forever when bad things happen, or we can stand tall, look for a way out, and see how God can turn something bad into something good.

When my hope became shaky, faith restored my hope. A magnitude of blessings came out of my trial. Whatever you are going through, turn your eyes toward the mindset of how God can use your trial for good. Our journeys are tailor-made for God's purpose in our lives.

Be bitter, or turn a mad-thing into a glad-thing. You get to choose.

• • •

If you would like to know more about HealInComfort, to order shirts, or to get in touch with Cherie, please go to www.healincomfort.com. To learn more about Cherie's 501(c)3, GiftingCare, to donate, or to have a HealInComfort shirt donated, visit GiftingCare.org.

THERE IS
ALWAYS
HOPE

Each of the stories in this book is proof that
Your Story Matters.
YOU matter to God.
He created you for a purpose.

Allowing Him into your story changes you and in turn, opens
the space for you to give. You can change your community,
your country, and the world. You WILL find peace and joy
every day as you step into your purpose and liberally give.

My prayer for you is that:

"You will be rich in every way
so that you can be generous on every occasion,
and through us your generosity will result in
thanksgiving to God."
2 Corinthians 9:11 (NIV)

"Owning your own story is the bravest thing you'll ever do."
Brene Brown

RESOURCES OF HOPE

From the Women of
There is Always Hope

Emra Smith
There is Always Hope
Your Story Matters
InternationalSchoolofStory.org
EmraSmith.com

Holly Dowling
A Celebration of You, an iTunes podcast
HollyDowling.com

Kathy Walters Burnsed
Beating the Clock: Managing Time God's Way
PerfectTimingToday.com

Juliet Van Heerden
Same Dress, Different Day: A Spiritual Memoir of Addiction and Redemption
JulietVanHeerden.com

Linda Znachko
He Knows Your Name: How One Abandoned Baby Inspired Me to Say Yes to God
HeKnowsYourName.org

Rachael Kathleen Hartman
Called to Write, Chosen to Publish: 20 Inspirational Thoughts for Christian Writers
Facing Myself: An Introspective Look at Cosmetic Surgery
OurWrittenLives.com
RachaelKathleenHartman.com

Angelena Cortello
Angel: The True Story of an Undeserved Chance
Healing Letters: A 140 Day Journey of Healthy Living

Courtney Santana
Off Kilter
Survive2Thrivefoundation.org

Karen Pearson
KarenJPearson.com

Cathy Rodgers
A Life Course of Miracles and Prayer: Supernatural Events in Ordinary Lives
CathyChats.com

Juanita Kretschmar
"Whole Health 'N Joyful News: Christ is Coming!"
Radio Broadcast on 95.7 FM
WHNJ.org

Sarah Huxford
The Harley Chronicles: Everything I Learned about my Marriage on the Back of a Harley
SarahHuxford.com
CompassionChristian.com

Pam Wolf
Finding Your Sweet Spot. Identity and Destiny – 7 Steps to a Purpose-filled Life
IdentityAndDestiny.com
TomAndPamWolf.com

Ingrid Vanderveldt
EBW2020.com

Natalie Phillips
@AudioDrPhillips on Twitter
Connect4Excellence.com

Regeanie Corona
AdvanceTheSeed.org
Abizstrategies.com
Regeanie.com

Cherie Matthews
HealInComfort.com
GiftingCare.org

APPENDIX

SMART GOALS

SMART Goals are based on the following attributes by Peter Drucker:

S pecific
M easurable
A chievable
R ealistic
T ime-Based

Follow this example to write down one goal.
Goal: "I would like to lose weight."
If all you do is think and say your goal, chances are it won't happen. Let's break down our sample goal into a **SMART** goal.

Specific: I would like to lose 10 pounds before my birthday.

Measurable: I will follow a healthy diet. I will eat protein (lean meats, fish, and legumes 5x a week; lean red meat 2x a week). I will keep three-quarters of my plate vegetables. I will eat fruit two times a day. I will keep nuts for snacks twice a day. I'll drink 8 cups of waters a day. I will exercise by walking three miles three times a week, on Tuesday, Thursday, and Saturday.

Achievable: Do I have the time and finances available to plan healthy meals? Do I have time in my schedule to exercise?

Realistic: Can I complete my goal? What is realistic for me? What do I need to say no to? How do I plan to eat at upcoming events and activities I've committed to? Think ahead.

Time-Based: If my birthday is in two months, I should be realistically able to complete my goal. If my birthday is next week, I won't be able to. What adjustments do I need to make?

Once you write out your **SMART** goal, it becomes easier to stick to. Before you go to bed, write out the next day's specific plan out. You pre-program your brain to make the choices you want to make. Situations, feelings, cravings, and circumstances will no longer control you.

ACKNOWLEDGMENTS

So Thankful

For Jesus, the beloved of the Father who empowers me by His Holy Spirit. He changes me, grows me, and fills me. It is truly an adventure to walk with God, to allow Him into my story, and watch Him share His story through mine. There is nothing quite like it!

"I will give thanks to you, Lord, with all my heart;
I will tell of all your wonderful deeds."
Psalm 9:1 (NIV)

For my supportive, fun, and creative husband, Roberdy. You stay steady and strong, yet flexible and accommodating, as I plunge into each next step of my Call. You are my rock, my joy, and my love.

For my daughters, Lianro and Candice. My love for you has no boundaries.

For my girlfriends, Carol Ogle and Vinetta Willis. Carol painstakingly, without complaint, edited each word and story. Vinetta, as my prayer partner, carried me through this journey. You are both a part of my heart forever.

For each of the incredible women in this book who graciously shared their stories with courage to empower and stir our souls with lasting HOPE. I love, adore, and treasure you.

ABOUT THE AUTHOR

EMRASMITH
YOUR STORY MATTERS
INTERNATIONAL SCHOOL OF STORY

Emra Smith is an inspirational challenger and facilitator of HOPE. She is a Speaker, Author, Corporate Trainer and Life Coach facilitating change.

Emra is a Certified Coach through Coach Training Alliance. She has successfully completed Licensure and Specialty-Certification as a New Life Story® Wellness Coach. Her expertise in the psychology and neuroscience of coaching extends her considerable experience in Life Coaching.

Emra is also a Facilitator for Identity & Destiny – Discovering God's Purpose for your Life, and the Director of Empowerment Circles Globally for EBW2020, Empowering a Billion Women by 2020.

Emra started speaking and teaching as a teenager in her church, and continued to speak throughout her Marketing and Sales career.

She became a Corporate Trainer in the Hospitality Industry and further specialized in Customer Service and various Human Resource training. Emra speaks to various organizations and churches and has won numerous awards and contests at Toastmasters.

Emra has differentiated herself through her unique and powerful inspirational speaking which she pours into any each topic and training.

She is the Founder and CEO of the International School of Story, a Place and Platform where women give and receive HOPE, empowered to boldly step into their stories. Emra is creator of the HOPE Doll Project and HOPE Campaign.

For continued inspiration and inspiring stories, fill out the HOPE Survey, and recieve your FREE ebook, *Complaint Free Living* at www.emrasmith.com.

For more about *The International School of Story* and to be a part of the global platform where women share HOPE through stories and learn from one another, visit www.internationalschoolofstory.org.

For products to share HOPE, to be encouraged, and to learn more about the HOPE Doll Project, visit www.HopeDoll.com.

To invite Emra to speak, host a workshop or training, to begin coaching with her, or to share your story, contact her at emra@emrasmith.com.

INTERNATIONAL SCHOOL OF STORY